Old World Daughter,
NEW WORLD MOTHER

ALSO BY MARIA LAURINO

Were You Always an Italian?

Old World Daughter,
New World Mother

AN EDUCATION IN LOVE & FREEDOM

Maria Laurino

W. W. Norton & Company

New York • London

For information about permission to reproduce selections from this book,
write to Permissions, W. W. Norton & Company, Inc.,
500 Fifth Avenue, New York, NY 10110

For information about special discounts for bulk purchases, please contact
W. W. Norton Special Sales at specialsales@wwnorton.com or 800-233-4830

Manufacturing by Courier Westford
Book design by Judith Stagnitto Abbate, Abbate Design
Production manager: Devon Zahn

Library of Congress Cataloging-in-Publication Data

Laurino, Maria.
Old World daughter, New World mother : an education
in love & freedom / Maria Laurino.
p. cm.
ISBN 978-0-393-05728-7 (hardcover)
1. Laurino, Maria. 2. Laurino, Maria—Family. 3. Italian Americans—Biography.
4. Italian American women—Biography. 5. Mothers and daughters—United
States—Case studies. 6. Children of immigrants—United States— Case studies.
7. Intergenerational relations—United States—Case studies. 8. Italian Americans—
Ethnic identity—Case studies. 9. Feminism—United States—Case studies. I. Title.
E184.I8L37 2009
306.874'3—dc22

2008035135

W. W. Norton & Company, Inc.
500 Fifth Avenue, New York, N.Y. 10110
www.wwnorton.com

W. W. Norton & Company Ltd.
Castle House, 75/76 Wells Street, London W1T 3QT

1 2 3 4 5 6 7 8 9 0

FOR TONY AND MICHAEL

$\mathcal{A}$ND, WHAT WAS EVEN MORE EXCITING, she felt, too, as she saw Mr. Ramsay bearing down and retreating, and Mrs. Ramsay sitting with James in the window and the cloud moving and the tree bending, how life, from being made up of little separate incidents which one lived one by one, became curled and whole like a wave which bore one up with it and threw one down with it, there, with a dash on the beach.

VIRGINIA WOOLF

$\mathcal{M}$EMORY TRULY COUNTS—for an individual, a society, a culture—only if it holds together the imprint of the past and the plan for the future, if it allows one . . . to become without ceasing to be, to be without ceasing to become.

ITALO CALVINO

Contents

Glassed In

$\mathcal{A}$ FEW SUMMERS AGO I found myself alone in a glass shop in Venice surrounded by thousands of dollars worth of unenclosed handblown jewelry. The owner had left me there, trusting my honesty.

He was a sweet-faced man whose life seemed bathed in the heat of softened canes of glass and just-made espresso. I admired the voluptuously colored pendants that he created in his small shop, sweltering from the August air and the steady gas flame, as he practiced a family trade that dated back to Murano glassmaking in the fourteenth century. He spoke English well, so we began a conversation. I learned that he was married to an American woman and they had a baby. Discussing life in Italy, I told him that my grandparents were born in the south of the country.

"Oh, they are much more traditional in the south than we are here in the north," he replied. "Family, for instance, is still very important to them."

As I fingered the pendants and bracelets before me, the phone rang and the glassmaker spoke rapidly and animatedly in Italian.

"*Mamma, vuoi un café?*" I overheard him say. Then he darted out with a small cup in his hand, looking back over his shoulder to ask if I could wait a few minutes.

"I'm sorry," he apologized upon his return. "I had to bring a coffee to my mamma."

Daughters

Basement Memories

HOW A YOUNG MARIA LEARNS OF THE OLD WORLD
WAYS OF HER GRANDPARENTS

I AM A DESCENDANT of people who believed in the primacy of family, who understood that the greatest moral, spiritual, and emotional satisfaction is derived from caring for others, especially the young and the old. They also believed in the evil eye and kept women out of the basement for fear that their menstrual cycle would spoil the fermenting wine. Most rational granddaughters would run for the hills (or from the suburbs) to escape this peasant past, and for many years I did just that.

The idea that my maternal and paternal grandfathers, both of whom died before I was born, pressed grapes in their New Jersey basement or backyard only confirmed my belief that I was some kind of Italian-American Beverly Hillbilly, plunked down in the middle-class section of the affluent suburb Short

Hills. Back in the Seventies (to add to the layers of my ethnic shame), Italian-American culture was defined by Francis Ford Coppola's *The Godfather*, not Francis roaming his extensive Napa vineyards and bottling his own brand of wine.

But as my mother liked to tell me, three decades earlier my grandfather Natale would bring home heavy wooden crates, shipped in refrigerated freight cars from the rolling hills of California to the train yards of Newark, New Jersey, filled with boxes upon boxes of rich purple grapes. Every October marked Natale's annual pilgrimage to the bustling Avenue C rail yards, where he would stand among crowds of Italian men tasting dozens of bunches of grapes. He would purchase about seventy crates containing hundreds of pounds of grapes to produce three or four barrels of wine, enough to last him until the next fall. My grandfather kept the grapes in his basement, along with a wine press, the oak barrels, and a trough that held several five-gallon glass jugs of his finished product sealed with a thick cork.

Like many southern Italian immigrants, my grandfather came to America at the turn of the twentieth century; he started his own construction company in 1906. He laid down the red bricks for a three-story apartment building at 1977 Springfield Avenue in Maplewood, making a home for his family along a busy road that led to the city of Newark. Although New Jersey didn't have the right climate for harvesting grapes, like the vineyards he had known in Conza della Campania, the small village in the province of Avellino where he was born, my grandfather found relief from the hot pavement by planting a flower and vegetable garden in a large lot he owned adjacent to his apartment building.

Natale, despite earning his bread through hard physical labor, needed roses, too, and he searched for a glimpse of beauty and a space for leisure in his life. He grew himself a fig tree and dug it up every winter, blanketing its roots like a baby until the chilled earth warmed at planting time. In summer, he'd pluck a leaf from one of his basil plants, roll the earthy, mint-scented herb tight, and tuck it behind his ear. A rose-covered trellis decorated the center of the garden, and water lilies floated in a goldfish pond. Colorful patches of pansies, poppies, peonies, and mountain pinks caught the interest of passersby. Although my grandfather never intended to part with his favorite flowers, he liked to please those who requested bouquets, so he put together bunches to sell for a quarter.

Early each morning my grandmother, Maria Cantarella Conti, entered the garden that her husband tenderly cultivated. Straddling the zucchini, squash, peppers, and dandelions, she would slowly squat her heavy body to the earth, pick the day's selection, and place it in her large apron pockets. Weighed down with these vegetables, my grandmother would waddle to the tomato vines to pluck a handful, then climb three flights to the kitchen to begin her morning cooking. Peering out the window, she'd usually catch a neighbor sneaking into my grandfather's garden to dig up dandelions for her family's dinner salad, but she kept the woman's offense to herself.

Rolling and cutting dough for ravioli, scooping out the ricotta cheese, tipping cans of olive oil that she grew tired of lifting all morning, dicing tomatoes and the garden vegetables, my grandmother worked tirelessly while her daughters mostly watched. In the small kingdom of her kitchen, she wished to keep the act of cooking for herself, and she was anxious when her children were near the stove's gas flames. My grandmother stretched the ravioli dough and rolled it nearly the length of the kitchen table. She spread a moist yellow sheet with a thin layer of ricotta cheese before placing another sheet of dough on top. My mother and her sister pinched closed each ravioli, the one and only cooking job they were assigned. But they would get nowhere near the crackling hot olive oil, succumbing early on to a fear of frying.

Meanwhile in the basement, my grandfather unloaded the crates of grapes he had purchased to begin his annual winemaking ritual. Although he must have missed harvesting his own fruit—partaking in that mystical communion between man and nature, earth and time of which winemakers speak—he set down to work with the juicy bunches picked from the other side of his vast new country. His crimson-stained hands marked the start of a months-long process—crushing grapes, straining pulp, and fermenting the juice—to ensure that there would always be wine with the meal.

· · ·

To TRAVEL to Maplewood today, that Philip Roth territory of upper-middle-class striving in *Goodbye, Columbus*, is to see streets filled with SUVs, Hondas, and minivans laden with children's car seats and athletic gear. It's hard to imagine that an ancient Mediterranean culture once laid down its New World roots here. But the Old World it was, with women making *mal'occhio*, the evil eye, against neighbors who had wronged them, chasing escaped pigs up Springfield Avenue, and capturing eels that had slithered out of filled kitchen sinks onto the floor. Even my grandmother was declared a witchy woman, a maker of the *maloyke*, as they said in their southern dialect. Poor woman: All she did was comment one bright Sunday morning on how handsome a husband and wife looked walking out of church together; when the man dropped dead the following week, all eyes were upon my grandmother.

Olive oil was as plentiful as basement wine, and women poured it freely and inventively over the body as well as into the cooking pot. An old woman from the neighborhood, as worn and withered as a garden root, was known for her dark brown hair. My mom, who began to gray in her late twenties, decided one day to seek out this oracle of the follicles for some advice.

"How does your hair stay so dark and shiny?" my mother inquired.

"I've never washed it," the woman replied. "I put olive oil on it."

When my mother, Connie, and her sister, Natalie, reminisce about the old days, they most often speak of their father. Their memories are colored as bright as his garden flowers. Both daughters, now in their eighties, still lovingly talk about the three-foot zucchini—*gagoots*, as they call them in dialect—that he grew and dried. How my grandfather cleaned every type of fish, invited neighbors over for banquet-size meals (okay, my grandmother did all the cooking), and tended his beloved garden. How he'd sit at the bedside of his daughter who was fighting a fierce childhood infection before the use of antibiotics, holding her hand and offering his remedy, a hot toddy made with tea and a shot of one of his homemade liqueurs.

Listening to these stories, the same ones told over and over in the rose-colored cadence of selective memory, I, too, become sentimental with the most primal of longings, to have what is gone and can never be retrieved. I erase the sadder stories of parental disappointments, turbulent marriages, and the inevitable domestic battles that would ensue in this home that my grandfather built. I tuck away the darker markers of Old World inheritance so steeped in custom, so frightened of individuality that for years my grandmother wouldn't address her first granddaughter because they didn't share the same name. (In Italian families, firstborn sons and daughters are supposed to be named after their grandparents.)

Even the shrewdest of critics, the most certain of writers can become a hopeless romantic when describing peasants and common folk, whose way of being challenges the assumptions of modernity—that life moves forward through progress, and progress is always benign. In her classic work *Black Lamb and Grey Falcon*, Rebecca West describes a Yugoslavian village in which half the population is illiterate: "They had found some way to moderate the flow of life so that it did not run to waste, and there was neither excess nor famine, but a prolongation of delight."

That's how I have come to think today about those hours in the dim light of the basement—as a prolongation of delight. I imagine a grandfather I never met helping navigate the flow of life through the making of wine, that anesthetizer of pain, dissolver of grief, bringer of happiness, if but temporarily. Yet embracing this story means recognizing its corollary, that the Old World way of life insisted that women assume a certain place in the natural order. And woman's place in that order excluded her from the basement.

According to my cousin Nat, the firstborn grandchild, my grandfather believed that if a woman was menstruating, her unclean state would upset the grapes' delicate process of fermenting and cloud the wine. Nat's stories are woven from memory, but if his recollections are right, my grandfather must have believed that the potent female fertility cycle gave women mystical and dangerous powers. My grandfather, with a pickax often in hand—"cement and stone works of all kinds" read his business card—was a man solidly of the earth. So, rather than having to look to the moon and consider the effects of its twenty-nine-day rotation on the cycles of the women in his family, he just kept all of them out.

Nat, on the other hand, practically lived in the basement. His rosy cheeks and devilish grin must have delighted my grandfather, who loved to make up rhymes about their shared name in his southern Italian dialect. Natale taught Nat how to crush grapes, scrape out the inky insides of walnut shells for a sweet liqueur, and cover the wine barrels with screening and cloth. And Nat happily stayed by Natale's side, escaping the demands of his overprotective mother and tempestuous father, my mother's brother.

Natale's infectious love of life provided a kind of background symphony to the workings of the house and, like the intricate notes of a cantata, lifted the spirits of all those around him. When my grandfather died suddenly of a heart attack on Mother's Day in 1946, his grief-stricken wife, whose children were by now grown and raising their own families in their parents' apartment building, refused ever to cook again.

Ten-year-old Nat—called "Natty-boy" by everyone in the family—proved himself young, brave, and innocent enough to challenge the unfair death of a fifty-seven-year-old man. As my grandfather's coffin sat in the parlor of their apartment, late one night Nat decided to climb in to end this awful slumber. He squeezed the waxy embalmed hands of the man who knew him best.

"Wake up, Grandpa, wake up!" he cried.

Finally he crawled out brokenhearted and frightened, and feeling betrayed. He was forced to accept a bleaker life alone in the basement. While the train yards beckoned others to taste the sweet California grapes, the jugs in the basement were never replenished. The family's old jelly jars, which served as wineglasses, were refilled instead with store-bought wine.

Yet even in the face of grief, my cousin Nat—"God bless him," my mother would say—has always defined industriousness. Through hard work, stamina, and inventiveness, he often managed to channel his sadness and anger into a positive result. Several months after my grandfather died, Nat realized that he alone knew about the five-gallon jugs of ready-to-drink wine that remained untouched in the cellar.

But getting to the wine, removing the tightly fitted cork, and lifting the heavy jug at first seemed impossible for a young boy—until Nat noticed an unused enema bag hanging on a wall in the basement. The bag was a reminder of the detested weekly ritual in which his mother forced Nat to lie on his side and have a tube shoved up his rear and warm water pumped into intestines that seemed ready to burst. So Nat came up with a plan, and made his next move with the skilled hands of a seasoned player in a crap game.

With his pocketknife, Nat sliced off the rubber hose attached to the enema bag, as well as the plastic nozzle at the other end of the hose. He drilled a hole into the dense cork of the wine jug, and another hole into the wooden trough, and ran the rubber hose, thick as a pinkie, into the jug and outside the trough. He clamped a metal clip tightly on the hose.

After school, Nat needed no sweetshop for an afternoon treat. Instead, he entered the basement and went directly to the trough. By releasing the metal clip and sucking hard on the bent hose, he created a siphon. Once the wine started to flow, he held the tube level with the liquid in the jug and filled up an empty Royal Crown soda bottle. Carrying cigarettes made from my grandfather's rolling machine, vegetables picked from the garden, and the homemade wine, Natty-boy climbed the fire escape ladders to the building's roof. This Italian-American Huck Finn leaned back on the tarry surface with a scallion dangling between his teeth, surveying the drifts in the current of traffic along Springfield Avenue.

· · ·

*A*T OUR kitchen table, there was never a mention of wine flowing through an enema tube or, heaven help us, anything vaguely sexual, like the fanciful theories about women and the winemaking process. Almost all the family stories were told by my mother, and these tales usually signaled that the simple joys of her childhood had disappeared.

As I grew older, my mother's banquet-size memories were

enough to send me straight out of the kitchen into the solitude of my small bedroom. (I preferred to imagine myself alone among the nighthawks of America in the shadowy stillness of an Edward Hopper diner.) In the quiet of my own room, I wrote down and stared at the words that supposedly defined me: Italian-American. And from those words emerged images that confused and haunted me, so strange and foreign were they to the life that I desired: basement wine, mammas in the kitchen making ravioli, corpses in the parlor, olive oil on unwashed hair, the deadly power of a greeting and a stare.

I made the hyphen in Italian-American into an arrow. I planned to become fully American, an enlightened twentieth-century woman, tossing back my shampooed hair and laughing at the notion that these ancient codes of behavior could in any way shape or influence me.

Other Mothers

HOW THE CULTURE OF THE MAMMA
IS REJECTED FOR MORE THRILLING POSSIBILITIES

*W*HEN I WAS a little girl, the small paradise of my grandfather's garden had already been paved; the new owners put up a parking lot. Deceased loved ones were laid out in funeral homes, not living rooms, and children climbed onto jungle gyms, not inside of coffins. Boys did not become men at the tender age of ten. In the blink of twenty years, the peasant culture that bustled with life in my grandfather's building—the homegrown garden; thick wooden wine barrels; and livestock slaughtered in the basement, with all parts consumed, from feet to blood frozen for pudding—had been permanently sanitized and replaced by supermarkets, liquor stores, and modern American life.

And so, too, shifted the family's division of labor. Without the need to build our own home, grow vegetables, make wine, or kill an animal before cooking it—jobs performed by the men in the family—the bulk of strenuous domestic duties went to my mom. My dad headed to work in a suit and tie to put food on the table. Even as a young girl I knew that his job commanded a respect far greater than housecleaning and child rearing. Whereas he inhabited the public world of commuter trains and a downtown New York office, my mother's private world was intimate, bound to the needs of her children and her husband—so much so that when my mother spoke about "the other mothers" in our town, the phrase suggested separateness rather than community. "Oh, the other mothers drive" meant that she was mostly confined to the house and dependent on my father to take her around on weekends. "The other mothers are on the PTA" signaled her insecurity about joining organizations where she might be the only woman without a college degree. Or, simply, "The other mothers are not like me."

The last statement was a complicated one. Contained in those few words of heartfelt difference were a meditation upon the influence of culture, the impediments to assimilation, and, perhaps ultimately, the decision to see the world as either a rational or an irrational place.

"The other mothers are not like me."

And she was right. The other mothers didn't knock on wood throughout the day; the other mothers didn't read omens from dreams into daily life; the other mothers might go to church, but their dressers weren't lined with votive candles and statues of the Virgin Mary, St. Anthony, St. Francis, and St. Joseph, and Jesus enclosed in a glass dome with dried carnations at the foot of his cross that had been carried home from Mother's Day masses. And they didn't have dressers with bottles of holy water in the drawers.

The other mothers never seemed to worry if their children weren't within sight at all times. My mother supposed that the children of those other mothers were watched over by a guardian angel, protecting them from all the hidden dangers in the world.

Who were the other mothers? Women whom I thought of as American. Mostly Irish Catholic and Protestant, they heated up Chef Boyardee for dinner, shopped at Lord & Taylor, drove to the hairdresser, and went out with their husbands on Saturday evenings, leaving their children with a babysitter.

My mother preferred not—not to serve canned ravioli, not to get her hair done or shop in department stores, not to drive, not to leave her children with anyone but a family member. My mother would not be American in the way that her daughter wanted her to be. (Dye your hair and serve Chef Boyardee, please!)

Tight family finances determined many of these decisions, but my mother would also not allow herself to indulge in personal pleasures. She would celebrate small moments: The completion of her housework and baking called for a cup of tea or a glass of chilled Gallo wine, depending on whether the day felt whole or cracked like the bread dough eggs. Most days she chose wine. She'd sit at the table sipping wine that matched the claret-colored robe of Bishop Fulton J. Sheen, faintly smiling from the creased and glossy photo on the cover of the paperback to which she returned each afternoon. But to find pleasure in life other than from a glass of wine and the words of a priest was ultimately more than she could handle.

My mother changed her name from Concetta to Constance, or Connie, when she went to school, but in womanhood she assumed the full freight of her proper name, accepting how, in Montaigne's words, "Constancy's part is played principally in bearing troubles patiently where there is no remedy."

Every daughter must wonder what her mother would have been like if another turn in the road had been taken. I'm sure my mother never imagined that marriage and motherhood would catapult her back to her ancestor's fate, sentencing her to a life of sadness and disappointment. When my grandfather died suddenly, my parents were still newlyweds delighted by the news of my mother's quick pregnancy. Four months later, the doctor was absent during a crucial moment in my mother's difficult delivery, and the newborn, dazed by his world's welcome, searched for oxygen in the stranglehold of the umbilical cord. My brother Henry was born mentally retarded. Cruelty ticked with the second hand, the loss of a minute's air bringing a lifetime of despair.

At age one, Henry had a soaring fever that wouldn't abate, and he experienced his first of a lifetime of seizures. My mother feared that her inability to control his fever worsened his condition, never fully accepting that his neurological problems stemmed from his birth trauma. It was one of many incidents reinforcing the guilt she has carried since my brother's birth. As a boy, Henry had to be watched constantly because running too fast or playing too hard could provoke a seizure.

Over the next thirteen years, my mother would have two more children—my brother Bob, then me. But her heart would always be broken over her first son's disability, and anguish and fear shadowed her maternal pleasures. To feel pure joy in child rearing was a perjury in our family court.

In some ways my brother's retardation became a metaphor for our family. It was a roadside barrier to the rapid-fire assimilation expected of second-generation Americans, slowing down our understanding and acceptance of New World values, especially the glorification of individual freedom. The cruel turn of fate in the delivery room encouraged my parents to carry forth, not abandon, the nineteenth-century southern Italian values upon which they were raised.

Perceiving the world as a very dangerous, not a welcoming, place, they reaffirmed the notion that the only people one could ever really trust were members of the family, and concomitantly that the family, not outside institutions, must take care of its own. My parents retreated, feeling self-conscious and embarrassed by my brother's endless repetition of the same thought or phrase and his failure to understand social cues. They rarely socialized, although they did welcome relatives—those who would best understand our problem, or *ou why* in their dialect—into our home.

Growing up, I was used to the loving, cooking, and wisdom of Italian mothers ("Trust only the family"; "Blood is thicker than water"; "Don't spit in the air or it will come right back down on you"), but suburban life always felt thoroughly topsy-turvy when the Old World great-aunts came to visit our small split-level home painted white with peacock blue shutters. I felt a dizzying disconnection, as if I had been dunked in a barrel of basement wine and emerged with the deep purple lips and crooked smile of someone who had drunk heavily of another version of reality.

"Zit-Zee!" my mom would shout as great-aunt Antoinette slowly hauled her ample body and thick-stockinged feet up our staircase.

"Coonjet-ah-gond!" my great-aunt would reply, as each affectionately addressed the other in dialect.

My grandfather Natale brought Antoinette, his half sister, to America when she was a young woman. It was an act of fraternal kindness because, in the unforgiving culture of southern Italy, my illegitimate great-aunt, the result of my great-grandfather's love of his wife's sister, could have been abandoned. When I think of Antoinette today, I can imagine our peasant past, the small stone shack in which my grandfather lived, the chickens that scurried in the backyard, the gatherings of women clad in black who sought laughter to hide their sorrow.

"Did you make any *tatalles*?" Aunt Antoinette would ask upon entering our kitchen.

"I don't have any fresh ones," replied my mom about her bread snack, *taralli*, made from a dough that is rolled into circles before being boiled, then baked to a crispy brown.

"That's okay," said Aunt Antoinette. "Give me the old ones."

My great-aunt was not fussy about food. She did odd things that reflected the poverty of her childhood, such as arguing with my mother over throwing out good leftovers, then picking out the remains from the garbage. Aunt Antoinette and my mother talked partly in English and partly in their southern dialect, which was incomprehensible to me.

"How's *Zooahjens*?" my mom would ask, uttering a name as baffling as the rest of the conversation.

"*Byejanzee*," said my great-aunt. Everyone seemed to have a *byejanzee*. The dialect word was derived from the Italian *pacienza*, and whatever caused the *byejanzee* usually required a patience and fortitude to deal with it beyond the capabilities of most human beings. Uttered with mourning and resignation, the word could sum up an entire conversation.

"Ah, *byejanzee*," my mother concurred, considering her own.

Great-aunt Giuseppina, small framed and quiet next to the boisterous Antoinette, comforted our kitchen with her calm, attentive nature. She and my mom exchanged recipes and intimacies like mother and daughter. Years later, when Giuseppina was dying of breast cancer, she wouldn't seek medical treatment. She assured my bewildered mother that she was bathing the lump every night with Witch Hazel, and believed it was getting better.

The older I grew, the more I recognized that age is not the only barrier between generations. My Old World relatives brought to our house their fears of medicine and modernity as well as their deep-rooted fatalism—that what happens in life is foreordained and ultimately out of our control. My favorite courier of this belief, delivering his message to our doorstep as faithfully as the postman in snow, rain, heat, or gloom of night, was my great-uncle Patsy, the brother of my maternal grandmother.

Having lived on both sides of the ocean, Uncle Patsy shrewdly assessed the events transpiring before him and captured their essence with unusual pith. This man of few words, all spoken in broken English, was not the kind of relative you would be anxious to introduce to other mothers, especially those who, unlike us, lived on the right side of the tracks—elegant, rich Short Hills residents raising budding debutantes. Yet we celebrated him as our family philosopher, or "philos" as he would have said, always chopping off the last syllables of his words. Uncle Patsy called himself a "compose" and sat in our kitchen singing his latest dirge, usually a lament on some aspect of modern life.

"I travel all over the coon-tree. I see a boy with a long-uh hair. To me he looks like a moon-key."

Beyond his musical aspirations (he even knew the barber who cut the singer Jimmy Rosselli's hair), Uncle Patsy's true savvy, the reason we called him a philosopher, was found in his response to life's standard greeting.

"How's everything?" my dad would ask knowingly, ushering Uncle Patsy into the living room.

"Ev-ah-ree-tings ah boolsheet."

A boy whose mother died of a hemorrhage after being forced by her husband to labor in the fields shortly after her stillbirth to twins, a boy subsequently raised by a cruel stepmother who could have been plucked from the pages of Grimm, Uncle Patsy intimately understood the continuum of human pain rooted in the arid soil of southern Italy. A construction worker, a "compose," and a "philos," he confronted daily the anguish of living, the bluff of life itself, filled with its phoniness, favoritism, and unfairness. He incorporated what most choose to deny, that all roads lead to the same place of disorder and decay, expressing the existentialist's dilemma in three simple words:

How's everything, Uncle Patsy?

Everything is bullshit.

• • •

$\mathcal{I}$NTEGRAL TO the American imagination, indeed a piece
of this country's constant and frenetic energy, is the notion that
the incriminating evidence on the tape can be easily erased, and
those little separate incidents that make up a life will dissipate
into the atmosphere, untraceable. That we are marked genetically and culturally, and the impact of these traits hovers over us
throughout life, does not fit into the founding myth of this nation
of immigrants, which urges us to believe that freedom, progress,
and a God-given right to happiness define our identity.

All I need do is look to Italy today to find characteristics
from which I wished to break loose while growing up. Italians,
inheritors of feudalism and Fascism, throw up their hands
like Uncle Patsy to the ludicrousness of controlling one's fate.
When a recent global research poll asked people to respond to
the statement "Success in life is pretty much determined by
forces outside our control," a large majority of Italians agreed.
Americans, on the other hand, overwhelmingly disagreed,
reaffirming the belief that we are self-directed individuals who
can shape our own destiny.

Italians assume that political and social connections most
often determine the course of a life, and they recognize the
constraints that family responsibilities place on personal ambitions. They scoff at Americans' boundless naiveté, that we can
handle everything we desire—from having large families while
both parents work full-time to insisting upon low taxes and
a limited role for government because individuals can best
take care of themselves. To the Italian mind, having it all is a
charmingly quaint proposition.

Navigating the ruins of the past on their daily cappuccino run, Italians recognize that ancestral attitudes can't be erased in a century or two. Madonna and child, that sacred notion of motherhood, translucent as a Raphael portrait, looms large in the national psyche. To be a mother inherently means to sacrifice a piece of oneself for another; this is not an option that a woman can turn off and on depending on her mood or liking. It is perhaps this interpretation of motherhood, as well as a woman's obligations to care for her aging parents and in-laws, that has helped turn Italy, the land that once defined *la famiglia*, into a country that now has one of the lowest birth-rates in the world.

The all-embracing mammas surrounding me as a child, as opposed to the other mothers I knew, still exist in the Italian consciousness. Known as a *mamma del sud*, a mother born in, or inheriting the traits of, the impoverished southern part of the country, she is fiercely protective, terribly fearful, histrionic, and utterly devoted.

"*Sta attenta!*"—Be careful!—the *mamma del sud* shouts throughout the course of the day, seeing danger in every crevice and corner of life. Her shriek rings as loudly as the toll of neighboring church bells if her precious *bambino* tumbles off his bike. She greets the rising sun every morning to cook a three-course lunch instead of handing out a euro for the school cafeteria, for the *mamma del sud* will do anything for her child, especially her son.

She is the protagonist of folk tales, the brunt of jokes, like the young man in love with a beautiful woman who tells him to prove his devotion by cutting out his mother's heart and delivering it to her. The man follows her orders (a real *gedrool*, or cucumber head, as my relatives would say), but while running to his lover with his mother's heart, he trips over a log. As the young man falls, the heart hits the dirt, prompting his mother's voice, woven into the muscles of her broken heart, to ask, "Did you hurt yourself, my son?"

. . .

*H*EADING TO elementary school, I was careful to leave behind traces of Old World peasantry, ready to be greeted each day by old American battle-axes teaching me reading, writing, and the arithmetic of what counted most in the cultural hierarchy.

"Girls, do any of you know if your ancestors fought in the Revolutionary War?" my third-grade teacher, Mrs. Morris, asked us one morning as we were still stretching from sleepiness. A proud member of the Daughters of the American Revolution, Mrs. Morris was describing the honor of belonging to this society, and it was the girls' task to go home and find out whether they, too, could one day join.

I was learning the great story of America—of brave wars fought, triumphal willpower roused, and rugged individualism garnered on a perilous frontier. It is a narrative that Americans can call upon again and again to reaffirm our special sense of identity and independence.

That morning when Mrs. Morris queried the potential DAR recruits, I tentatively lifted my hand halfway. But when I asked my parents in the evening whether any of our relatives had fought in the Revolutionary War, they burst out laughing.

"They were probably picking grapes in Italy," my father replied.

I left the room, embarrassed by my ignorance and annoyed to have a grape-picking, not a musket-drawing, ancestry. True Americans were supposed to have fought in our great wars, trampling out the vintage where the grapes of wrath are stored. My family, on the other hand, had been storing grapes for the next vintage.

Needing to wash the feudalistic, wine-stained terrain of southern Italy out of my genes, I preferred to cross the bridge to the New World, easily accomplished with a slam of the screen door and a skip down the street to my best friend's house. There housework was a chore to be avoided, and my friend's young Irish-American mother listened to Helen Reddy's "I Am Woman," energized each time she picked up the phonograph needle and the single repeated. Closing her eyes, breathing in the melody, she stood dreamily while music filled the living room. Meanwhile, dishes were piled high on the kitchen counter as hardened egg yolks and the remains of beef and potatoes from the night before patiently waited to be scrubbed.

In my mother's and aunts' kitchens, I heard women roar—laughing or sparring over food, just cooked or disposed of. The chatter was shaped to the contours of domestic life, and children were always by their side. My mother was most at ease among these women who prepared a sauce, sautéed the meat, boiled the macaroni, and chirped like excited caged birds while the men sat on the porch brooding over the limits of freedom.

"One of them sits like this," Uncle Frank, who married my father's sister Bridget, reported one Sunday, describing the taciturn men of the family—my father and his oldest brother. He imitated my Uncle Jimmy reclining in a chair, head bowed to the left, rocking. "And the other sits like this," he said, mimicking my father, head bowed to the right.

"Peas in a pod," my mother replied.

"Can I please join the ladies?" asked Uncle Frank to a roomful of squeals and high-pitched laughter.

The ladies were needed to lighten the mood, which often turned dark in the company of the men. My father's brother Rocco would taunt his sister Ann, and sometimes their arguments became so heated that my father needed to intervene and separate the two.

"So what do you think you'll die of?" Uncle George, my mother's brother, asked everyone at our kitchen table on another Sunday afternoon, the family gathering day, posing the question as casually as checking in on the weather. "I know what it's going to be for me. My heart. Because I only have half a heart functioning."

I watched in amazement and dread as everyone guessed that day how their road would end. But the worst part for me was knowing that my mother would have to participate. I didn't want to hear her answer. I couldn't imagine life without her in the kitchen.

"Oh, I don't know, George, I guess my heart," she said. "As long as I go quickly. I always tell my children, whatever you do, don't ever put me in a nursing home."

My mother devoted herself to her family, and she expected that same devotion back. Her creations, food and children, even when neither came out as planned, kept her flying from room to room until evening. If she awoke feeling as limp as damp laundry, sheer will turned her as crisp as the sheets plucked from the clothesline later that day. She made dinner, washed the dishes, and brought out the cookies, cannoli, and coffee. Eat enough sugar and there's no time left to cry.

I was still too young to imagine the longings or desires of the Italian mothers or the other mothers whom I knew—how they coped with the *byejanzee* that life had dealt them, or what caused a salty tear to be shed along with the chords of a pop song. I did recognize, though, that the other mothers' kitchens were empty of Old World banter, and within those spaces of unwashed pots and pans, I detected a freedom absent from our lives.

The other mothers held a less tight reign over their children. Their daughters could walk to the local Roy Rogers for Sunday dinner, while I was never allowed to skip our weekly tradition of spaghetti and meatballs. The other mothers followed the Anglo-Saxon custom of sending children into the world like daring little Lewis and Clarks exploring and discovering, while my mother inherited the Mediterranean instinct to keep young and old close to home. Summer sleepaway camp and a junior high school trip to Greece during spring break were activities embraced and lauded by the other mothers. But not by my own.

"Miss Independent, here," my mom would remark each time I headed out. And with each step, I felt the weight of those words with their hint of ridicule and implication of my arrogance—the wayward daughter who chose friends over family.

Assessing American life with my youthful antennae, I soon homed in on the flip side of a culture that cherishes the family: the reluctance to offer wings to its children; the insistence on duty and respect, not freedom. My mantra in the confessional, first suggested by my mother when I was seven years old and terrified of what to tell the priest behind the closed wooden door, followed me through life, a nagging ache second-guessing all of my decisions: "Bless me father for I have sinned. I have disobeyed my mother and father."

The anti-individualist ethos at the center of the Italian-American household—that family members support and care for one another forever and then some—constantly bumped into my desire to forge a separate identity in an American culture that fostered the creation, and countless re-creations, of the self. Possessing the simple clarity held by only the young and the orthodox, I had no doubts about the path to my future. My mother's plight was too difficult, the private world too stultifying. We had a family member who could never aspire to independence, who would always need someone else's care.

As a teenager, I preferred spending time with my father. We could talk about our shared political beliefs; I inherited his admiration of Franklin Delano Roosevelt and his disgust with Richard Nixon, or Tricky Dickey, as we liked to call him. My father would shake his head, perplexed as to why so many Italian-Americans he knew, sons and daughters of pushcart vendors, electricians, and plumbers, became Republicans, abandoning the Democratic Party's historic alliance with the poor and the workingman. And I would nod along, delighted to be listening to my father, this man who seemed most comfortable alone. Content to sit back once the meal was done, lifting my feet above the wispy strands of my mother's agile broom, I was certain that a life centered around the kitchen would never be one to which I aspired.

It was the mid-1970s, and the "choice" presented to American women was embodied by two iconic television figures, June Cleaver and Mary Richards, played by Mary Tyler Moore. The radiant Fifties mother of two boys, June Cleaver wore pearls while she vacuumed. The beret-tossing Mary Tyler Moore ushered in the Seventies proving that a driven single woman was gonna make it after all. Given these archetypes, what studious and bright young woman wouldn't prefer to be enlightened, liberated Mary Richards?

At home, I had witnessed maternal obligations deeper and more terrifying than Cleaver's mere housework; I had heard the enduring ancestral call of sacrifice, and I was working hard to ensure that my mother's cup of wine would not be handed to me.

My mother sensed this desire in me, and her response confirmed my betrayal:

"*Marrone-a-mee! Madiucce*, you are getting very independent."

Age of Reason

How a college professor offers
feminism, rationalism, reason,
and (oops) authoritarianism

$\mathcal{I}$N MY SENIOR YEAR of high school, I eagerly signed up for courses that reflected the pressing issues of the day, such as Women in Literature, and I greedily fingered copies of *Ms.* magazine. Thinking of nothing else but college, I asked a friend one weekend whether she would drive me to Seton Hall University, a small school not far from where my mother had grown up. With high hopes that a visit to a local campus might be inspiring—and in one of the sorrier attempts to have fun on a Saturday night—we circled round and round the grounds, peering through my friend's car windows at lit and dark buildings. Unlike the loamy rewards of my grandfather's garden, my paradise was a paved parking lot.

Leaving home for college was taken for granted in the competitive, affluent suburb in which we lived, but always in the back of my head I knew my luck in being born my father's daughter, a man who valued education and earned a certificate in international trade from Rutgers University but never was able to complete the extra years he needed for a bachelor's degree. Instead, he would set aside enough savings to pay for as much education as his son and daughter sought.

A little more than a decade ago, a journalist writing a book about a case in which my brother Bob was a lead prosecutor asked me to lunch to learn more about my family. We talked over sushi and salad at a Japanese restaurant, and walking back to my office I mentioned as an afterthought that my father was a feminist.

"Oh, really," he said, sensing a good anecdote and searching his jacket pocket for a pen.

I explained how my father wanted me to attend any college that I chose and always supported my living away from home to pursue a career.

The journalist smiled politely and put back his pen. I realized how silly my explanation must have sounded to a politically engaged, socially conscious person. He had no idea how radical the concept of establishing an independent life was for a daughter in a traditional Italian-American family.

. . .

*T*HE WHOLE FAMILY packed and piled into our giant seven-year-old sauternes (I memorized the color from the car brochure) Sedan de ville Cadillac for our trip to Washington, D.C., and the start of my college career. Each stop on the turnpike signaled my further good-bye to slow-cooking sauce, crunchy *tatalles*, and vegetables seasoned with parmigiano cheese. Having rarely traveled outside of New Jersey, we got lost in Maryland and looped around the highway enough times to make me carsick. Tension pumped the air with the same start-and-stop motion as my father's foot riding the break, but my mother did her best to hide her sadness. I waved them all off shortly after we finally arrived in front of what would become my new home, St. Mary's Hall. *Santa Maria!* I cursed my lousy lot of being placed in the only all-girls' dorm on campus, and the only one named after a saint.

Despite my large dreams and big talk, I had never been away from home for more than one week. My proud entry through the main gates of Georgetown University's Gothic gray campus was short-lived. I cried my eyes out the first few nights, and I overate for the next few years.

My feelings of alienation, which always reemerged on Friday afternoons when the last class ended, escalated like a preheating oven reaching peak temperature on Saturday nights. Occasionally there was the party invitation: The boys hovered in the living room corners of a beat-up town house, a chip and dip spread of flaking paint and sagging beams capped with beer-stale air, yet still a prized possession compared to a dorm. The girls let loose in a circle dance of linked arms and pent-up energy, a swirl of flamingo pinks and kiwi greens that turned into a tropical frenzy when Billy Joel hammered our souls with his electrified piano strokes.

You Catholic girls start much too late, he crooned. They swooned, and I wanted out.

He was right, of course, but who admits this? Isn't college supposed to be about posture and artifice? About the freedom to find an original personality, to leave behind the rigid demands of an Italian Catholic upbringing and become the young woman you dreamed of while greedily fingering college catalogs on the bed in the house of your youth?

We had enterprising, socially minded female undergrads who challenged the Jesuit university's position on women's reproductive health and fought (unsuccessfully) to house a gynecological clinic on campus. But I avoided the topic altogether. I joined the alternative left campus newspaper and assumed the identity of girl reporter.

Just say notebook.

Like any teenager trying to find her way, I sought guidance from schoolgirls and scholars. Midway through my freshman year, I was introduced to a woman professor antithetical to all I knew. At fifty-two, she was five years younger than my mother and couldn't have been more different in background or style. Having grown up in Oklahoma, she was pure Americana, beginning her academic life at a small midwestern college, then transferring east to earn her bachelor's degree from Barnard and her doctorate from Columbia.

She was someone who replaced Uncle Patsy's worldview with Virginia Woolf's. Someone who didn't need to repeat "gold-in-my-ear" to remember the name Golda Meir. As a politically engaged leftist teenager, she had joined the Young People's Socialist League; she eventually became an academic who raised three children too.

Shouldn't every young woman, especially one reared by a *mamma del sud*, have a feminist role model?

Mine turned into a right-wing militarist prepared to topple totalitarian governments and support repressive authoritarian regimes.

And yours?

. . .

*E*NTERING COLLEGE in the late Seventies, I was a member of that privileged generation that reaped the benefits, without doing any of the grassroots work, of the feminist movement's radical challenge of the structure of American society and a workplace whose options had been primarily limited to the jobs of teacher and nurse. As Robert Reich noted in his book *The Future of Success*, in 1968 nearly 40 percent of women entering college said they wanted to become schoolteachers; by 1975 the number dropped to 10 percent, and the rate has remained about the same ever since.

Responding to the solitary despair of the housewife's stifling, unvarying days ("Yet somehow, as I buy All from these shelves / And the boy takes it to my station wagon, / What I've become / Troubles me even if I shut my eyes," contemplates the middle-aged woman in Randall Jarrell's "Next Day"), the feminist movement proposed an extraordinary idea—that women, personally and economically, could achieve parity with men. How this idea would manifest itself in a society structured on the principles of competition and profit, and what the ramifications would be—as obvious and important as these questions were—still remained largely unanswered. But one idea was certain: Parity could be closer at hand through the development of women's personal autonomy.

I absorbed this vital message, which was reflected in my choice of college heroines: a fictional medieval character; a brilliant, deceased twentieth-century writer; and a government professor in living color. Each offered, in print or in person, the possibility of autonomy.

My fictional heroine came to life in a class on Chaucer. I fell in love with the indomitable spirit of the Wife of Bath, and even tried to match the character's astrological chart (Taurus the bull dominated by Venus the love goddess) to my own April birth date. She was a famously difficult character in literature, considered by some a monstrous victim of misogynist culture and by others a cheeky representative of Chaucer's prescient feminism. I agreed with the latter, finding her a welcome antidote in the land of Billy Joel and giggling girls. I might have also felt at home with this red-wine-loving woman, having grown up with a few medieval characters of my own.

Her bawdy prologue in the *Canterbury Tales* was in part a response to the repressive writings of St. Jerome, who argued that marriage to women—a whiny, materialistic lot—was the basest form of male existence. Chastity, the highest virtue and calling, Jerome told us, reigned in paradise. The Wife of Bath responded by extolling the virtues of her sexual adventures with her five husbands. She countered her last husband's lengthy recitation of tales of wicked wives by asking, "Who painted the lion, tell me who?" referring to an Aesop's fable about a man who painted a picture of a man defeating a lion; in the fable, the lion remarks that he would have drawn the picture from his own perspective, one that defeated the man. Chaucer put on the table the Christian notion of the subordination of women, considered the natural order of life decreed by divine law, and had the Wife of Bath respond with humor, complexity, and contradiction.

The Wife of Bath's Tale poses the famous question that still haunts us today: What do women want?

The answer is revealed through the story of an errant knight who entrusts a crone to determine their future together. Because the knight ingeniously gives the decision-making power to the old woman, in effect giving her sovereignty, she turns into a beautiful maiden. Countless critics have interpreted the meaning of this fable, which can also be found in other medieval verse romances. Cultural historian Marina Warner sees the romance leading toward a "utopian destination—of negotiated exchanges, of generosity and trust. . . . Sovereignty over self—not over others; the right to govern one's own person, not the right to govern others."

Wommen desiren to have sovereynetee is the forward-looking message in the medieval tale.

Looking back on my college years, I can't think of another idea that I took more to heart, and these words defined my nascent feminism. Literature always served as my blueprint for life, and my architects of female autonomy were Chaucer's ribald genius and Virginia Woolf, the modern girl's essential heroine. A political scientist introduced me to Woolf's nonfiction. In a cramped office that barely fit a desk and a chair, I said hello to Jeane Jordan Kirkpatrick, whose taut face was framed by short-cropped wavy brown hair. My freshman government professor had suggested that I introduce myself to Kirkpatrick, whose reputation in the field was growing, so I asked to interview her for a newspaper story. After shutting my notebook, we began a more relaxed discussion, and she invited me to come back again.

As it turned out, Kirkpatrick frequently carved out time to see me, and she seemed genuinely interested in talking with a college student about feminism, motherhood, and her struggles against sexism in academia. Kirkpatrick's sometimes abrupt manner was softened by her absentmindedness. She could look betrayed by a variety of inanimate objects that managed to get the better of her, forever fiddling with a jingling key ring outside her office, unable to remember which key opened the door. Or searching for the university's label of a course she taught (I needed another political theory course to qualify for a government major), Kirkpatrick would rummage through drawers, tossing papers high in the air as she looked in frustration.

"Political theory—it must be political theory," she muttered, trying to act the role of advisor while pages of xeroxed forms fluttered to the floor.

Misplaced keys and floating papers, however, were minor interruptions to discussions that I found thrilling. It had been less than a year since I left behind the women in the kitchen, the other mothers, and the modestly self-assured high school teachers. I had watched the mothers exchanging recipes and tuning in to Mike Douglas, and the teachers penciling in favorable grades. The rhythms of housework, the seductive early morning aroma of Sunday gravy—these were the spheres of influence in which I saw women assert themselves.

Kirkpatrick, on the other hand, wove erudition, authority, and opinion into every breath, demanding from the listener a level of engagement that both excited and daunted. Routinely punctuating her thoughts with a "Not ah-tall," she transported me from a dreary office to a London parlor.

"We were fiercely intellectual," she said one afternoon, reminiscing about her undergraduate days at Barnard and pouncing on the word "fiercely" the way a jackal attacks its prey. Like the dark curly escarole that my mother added to an iceberg lettuce salad, Kirkpatrick could be a bitter green, but deeply satisfying nonetheless.

During one office visit, our discussion turned to Virginia Woolf. Kirkpatrick urged me to read *A Room of One's Own* and *Three Guineas*, Woolf's companion works about the intractable inequalities for the "daughters of educated men." Kirkpatrick, however, mostly dismissed the more radical *Three Guineas*, which Woolf published a decade later, moving beyond the question of female autonomy to a broader definition of feminism and urging women to do whatever is in their power to help fight fascist tyranny. By suggesting Woolf's nonfiction, Kirkpatrick handed me an essential feminist primer.

It's hard for a girl not to cherish Woolf's calm presentation and impassioned reasoning about the historic denial of basic human rights to women. But the title of her first feminist treatise literally hit home. Having grown up in a small house, I could never escape the fighting that centered around my brother and his severe emotional problems. Thin walls provided no refuge from the shouting, and my room, right next to his, felt like an annex of the battleground.

A room of one's own meant the solitude to dream and the choice of not having to deal with another person's overwhelming daily needs. But I had also begun to intuit that college freedom had the pristine yet artificial scent of a new car (sooner or later, coffee or life spills over), and I wondered how long I could preserve this message of female autonomy.

· · ·

ONLY WITH the benefit of hindsight, the distance of time, could I see how Jeane Kirkpatrick had influenced me, offering with conviction both rationalism and reason. For a while it felt as though our serendipitous first meeting had forever locked the door to the winemaking basement, with its crimson-stained troughs of Old World superstitions and traditions, opening instead a European salon illuminated by Enlightenment thinking. Kirkpatrick was my private symbol of that mighty Age of Reason, with its powerful insistence that science, freedom, and progress could counter the dark days of custom, faith, and fanaticism. No Witch Hazel touched the hands; no olive oil greased the hair of this political theorist. To spend time with her erased any last traces of mammas making *mal'occhio*.

At first Kirkpatrick shared with me the best of Enlightenment values—equality of the sexes, individual autonomy, and self-determination. Her feminism was about securing the same professional opportunities and individual rights as men. Bruised by the sexism that she had encountered when first applying for a university position in the Sixties, Kirkpatrick talked about the difficulties in establishing herself in a male field. A colleague explained—"very flatly, very openly," she recalled—" 'I'll tell you, Jeane, we don't hire women. We are more comfortable without women; we like it that way.' "

A decade later, when Kirkpatrick began researching her first book, *Political Woman*, about the legal barriers and social difficulties faced by women in state legislatures, she mentioned the project to Harold Lasswell, her mentor and a highly regarded political scientist. He responded, "But Jeane, you don't have a subject there."

Comments such as these may have fueled her early passion for social change, leading Kirkpatrick to conclude *Political Woman* with the sound and fury of a feminist manifesto: "For women to achieve de facto political equality, to enter political life in the same numbers as men and achieve the same levels of office as men, both a cultural and social revolution is required. Social goals, beliefs about the identity and the role of men and women, practices concerning socialization, education, political recruitment and family: all must be altered to support the accession of women to full participation in political power."

By finding a place for herself in the world while raising three sons, Kirkpatrick presented choices that I had never witnessed before. I still remember her unsentimental yet heartfelt response when I asked how raising children affected her work. I have three sons, she told me. I probably could have written a few more books if I didn't have all three. But how could I ever trade more books for my sons?

My mother, on the other hand, believed that life for women was either one way or the other: stay home in a housedress and raise a family, or be a fashionable single working woman, like her widowed, childless sister-in-law. My mother always felt guilty about reentering the workforce as a clerk typist to help pay for our college tuition. Although she sought to pass along her parents' values and liked me by her side, my mother, like all human beings, was conflicted. Part of her also longed for me to escape her fate, and she imagined that my interest in journalism could make me a high-powered Diane Sawyer type. My mom seemed genuinely perplexed when Sawyer, the ultimate working woman, decided to marry. "What did she see in that older guy?" she wondered about Mike Nichols.

Kirkpatrick offered even more, initially at least, championing the New Deal values that my family held dear, and peppering her progressive thoughts about women with quotes from Virginia Woolf. Although Kirkpatrick abandoned her socialist past before graduating from college—her grandfather was a founder of an Oklahoma socialist party in the early 1900s and taught his granddaughter that socialism was "more fair, the distribution of everything was more fair"—Kirkpatrick spent much of her life as a Humphrey Democrat. Her husband, Evron Kirkpatrick, fifteen years her senior, was Hubert Humphrey's first political science professor. As the years went by, she became more conservative, aligning herself with the "Scoop" Jackson, not George McGovern, wing of the Democratic Party.

When I asked Kirkpatrick whom she planned to support in the 1980 presidential election, she told me Teddy Kennedy, shrugging over the lack of plausible candidates. Her answer fit the Jeane Kirkpatrick whom I had come to know, and I printed it in a campus newspaper story—to the chagrin, I later discovered, of conservatives in the government department.

. . .

*I*F MY narrative of Jeane Kirkpatrick ended here—a private story of a college girl inspired by a woman professor who

successfully challenged the male academic hierarchy and published a book arguing that social goals, the identity of men
and women, and ideas about education and family needed to
be altered to support the ascension of women into political
life—I doubt that anyone would challenge the words "Jeane
Kirkpatrick" and "feminist" in the same sentence. But, of
course, her story is not private, and her surprising public narrative forced me to question the foundations of a feminism
that she helped lay out for me as a college student. A year
after Kirkpatrick told me that she was going to support Teddy
Kennedy, she became the first woman to serve as the United
States ambassador to the United Nations and a member of
Ronald Reagan's cabinet.

Reagan's appointment of Kirkpatrick was based on an essay
she had published in *Commentary* magazine called "Dictatorships
and Double Standards" that excoriated Jimmy Carter's foreign
policy, which she believed led to the toppling of the shah in Iran
and the growing support for Daniel Ortega and the Sandinista
movement in Nicaragua. Offering what she called "rationalism
and reason" in foreign policy, Kirkpatrick outlined the differences between totalitarian and authoritarian regimes. According to her worldview, the former were always intolerable, while
it was in the interest of the United States to support "friendly"
authoritarian ones. Her attack of Carter's policies made her the
darling of hawkish right-wingers, and a few months after the
article appeared she was introduced to Ronald Reagan.

By the time I graduated from college, Kirkpatrick, whose
prim and schoolmarmish appearances on Sunday morning
television shows earned her the Thatcherite sobriquet "iron
lady," became a visual symbol of the administration's decisions

to support El Salvador's military government and its infamous death squads, as well as the Nicaraguan contras. Student protestors at Berkeley poured fake blood onto a podium at which she tried to deliver a lecture on the history of American political values, and she was banned from other speaking engagements. Brown University history professor Joan Scott, the keynote speaker at the Berkshire Conference on the History of Women, explained that she excluded Kirkpatrick from this event because she was "not someone I want to represent feminine accomplishment."

The former U.S. ambassador is also absent from the *Handbook of American Women's History*, a reference guide found in college libraries that includes such figures as Madeline Albright and Billy Jean King. An editor's note explains: "Only those contemporary persons, events, and issues that the editor deemed crucial to provide critical background for the post-1960s phase of the modern women's movement have been included." Although breaking boundaries was a major criterion for admission, the editors decided that Kirkpatrick, who became the first woman foreign policy cabinet member, shouldn't share the same pages as a well-known tennis player.

Kirkpatrick was even accused of lacking a uterus. Among the many criticisms heaped upon her was a comment in a *New Republic* article by Naomi Wolf that described Kirkpatrick as having "a voice so Olympian, so neck-up and uninflected by the experiences of the female body, that the subtle message received by young female writers is: to enter public voice, one must abide by the no-uterus rule."

Watching this fierce reaction to my former professor, I became intrigued by the question, Can a conservative be a

feminist? After Kirkpatrick resigned from the Reagan administration in 1985, I decided to write a feature about her for the
Village Voice, where I was working at the time as a reporter. "I
have thought of myself as a feminist my entire life," Kirkpatrick told me, returning to the pages of Virginia Woolf's *A Room
of One's Own*, this time to describe the harsh ways in which
she had been treated by her male colleagues in government.

Despite months of interviewing dozens of thoughtful
women ("What feminism is all about is not helping a few
women with Ph.D.s and wine-colored briefcases," responded
Ann Lewis, then national director of Americans for Democratic Action), the question remained fundamentally unanswered. Yet outraged readers sent letters and columns to the
Voice; some feminists deemed me traitorous for even asking.
Although I personally agreed with the politics of the women
who opposed Kirkpatrick's positions—I was equally appalled
by her warrior vision—I had difficulty understanding the logic
of editing her out of a handbook of women's history. Kirkpatrick, who died in December 2006, was remembered in a
front-page *New York Times* obituary as one of the most powerful women in American history: "No woman had ever been
so close to the center of presidential power without actually
residing in the White House."

. . .

*T*ODAY, THANKS TO the movement's achievements, more
women have entered into positions of power, illustrating some
of the conundrums and contradictions in which contemporary feminism has found itself. At a forum I attended about

women's struggles to balance career and motherhood, a newspaper columnist cited George W. Bush's former communi-
cations director Karen Hughes as a model of success whose
resignation illustrated the pitfalls that women face even at the
highest levels of power. Condoleezza Rice, the first African-
American woman secretary of state, is invited by feminist fac-
ulty members at Ivy League universities to be their keynote
conference speaker. No one is throwing blood onto stages
on which she appears, nor has she received a metaphorical
hysterectomy. And it's doubtful that Rice would be excluded
from an updated version of the *Handbook of American Wom-
en's History*. But what are the ideological differences between
Rice, who also ascended to government power from academia,
and Kirkpatrick?

Feminism, of course, has evolved and changed over the
past forty years. Early feminist leaders were firebrands and
iconoclasts who paved the road for changes that benefited the
lives of women with more moderate views and temperaments.
And today, in an American landscape of seemingly unlimited
products for every consumer, feminism—we hear time and
again—is about giving women choices. But outside the fight
to protect a woman's right to terminate a pregnancy, that definition renders feminism virtually meaningless and politically
toothless.

It may be impossible to find an all-inclusive definition for
feminism because a woman's struggle to find a place in the
world is rooted in, and reflected by, the prism of her own experience. My inclination to tell the journalist that my father was
a feminist stemmed from knowing how unusual it was for an
Italian-American man of my father's generation (my dad was

born in 1915) to support and pay for his daughter's college and graduate school education. The journalist, however, who was Jewish and raised in a more progressive family, probably sought an anecdote about my dad as a grassroots organizer or participant in pro-choice rallies.

And a feminism that is chiefly about autonomy is bound to liberate one person at the expense of another. I'm sure that my mother, in charge of the child rearing and housework, would never have used the word "feminist" to describe my father. Professional women I know refer to their husbands as feminists because the men support their wives' career choices. But would the nannies employed by these upper-middle-class families, often scrambling to find care for their own children, call these same men feminists?

Virginia Woolf had the prescience in the Thirties to recognize the dangers of a feminism based solely on autonomy and equality. In *Three Guineas* she argued that after women's right to earn a living had been won, the word "feminist" should be thrown out of the language if its only meaning is "one who champions the rights of women." Within the paltry limits of this definition, "a dead word, a corrupt word" exists. If the word is destroyed, wrote Woolf, in the cleansed air we could see the task ahead: "Men and women working together for the same cause."

• • •

If Jeane Kirkpatrick had once represented for me the best of Enlightenment values, ultimately she revealed the worst of them too. She was my bright symbol of progress and reason amid the dim flames of Old World tradition, yet her fierce beliefs and ambition revealed the dangers of what cultural theorist Terry Eagleton calls "withered, anemic" reason: "just a set of mechanical procedures for calculating which means will most effectively secure your self-interested ends." Indeed, the thesis that briefly made her famous (or infamous)—that authoritarian dictators are "better" than totalitarian ones—fits Eagleton's definition of "withered reason."

If Kirkpatrick believed that illegally trading arms to Iran to support the Nicaraguan contras—a course of action she urged Reagan to adopt—was an example of "rationalism and reason" in foreign policy, her logic shows how far reason, that touchstone of Enlightenment values, can be stretched to its self-interested ends. Similarly, the feminist desire for autonomy, if taken to the extreme, can glue itself to withered reason like a gnat onto flypaper. A few years ago, a *New York* magazine article entitled "A Death of One's Own" argued that the suicide of writer and professor Carolyn Heilbrun was the final expression of a woman exerting individual choice. The decision of a healthy woman in her seventies to take her own life—to leave behind a husband, children, and grandchildren—the article reasoned, was justified by Heilbrun's feminism.

"Heilbrun's suicide was part of the plan she had all along, perhaps an essential component of her feminism," wrote Vanessa Grigoriadis in *New York* magazine. She quoted Heilbrun's work: "We women have lived too much with closure—there always seems to loom the possibility of something being over, settled, sweeping clear the way for contentment. This is the delusion of a passive life. When the hope for closure is abandoned, when there is an end to fantasy, adventure for women will begin."

Grigoriadis offered this conclusion: "And suicide, while on one level is closure, is a kind of freedom on another."

Gloria Steinem also conflated suicide with a powerful autonomy at Heilbrun's memorial service, comparing the writer's death to an African rain goddess, the queen of the Lovedu tribe who chooses at the end of her reign when to die. It is ironic that one of the founders of modern feminism chose this tribe to depict Heilbrun's courage, for anthropologists who have studied the Lovedu tell us that its men are permitted several wives and the sexes live in segregated quarters. Wives deliver food to the home of their husbands, where the men choose to eat anytime they wish. Husbands can beat their wives, and women can't visit their own relatives without permission from their husband or mother-in-law. Men have unfairly divided up the labor so the women must hoe, weed, husk, and pound grains while the men use plowing machinery. The queen knows that her reign must end by the ritual suicide ordained by her ancestors; she is robbed of a natural death.

I can only imagine that Steinem invoked the romantic and godlike metaphor of a rain queen to seek solace while grieving the loss of a friend. For Steinem in her 1979 essay "The Good News Is: These Are Not the Best Years of Your Life" argued that most women do not become radicalized until they reach middle and old age and see firsthand, outside the protected space of the ivory tower and once their children are grown, the inequality in their lives. She closed the essay with the optimistic suggestion, "One day, an army of gray-haired women may quietly take over the earth."

But this was not the case. Instead, a gray-haired feminist decided to quietly take her life.

What a terrifying trajectory for the future of feminism, and of humanity: that the sovereignty the Wife of Bath described centuries ago, the secret of what women most desired, could reach its modern-day conclusion through a woman's choice to end her life. To describe suicide as feminist freedom, the ultimate act of autonomy—rather than the product of depression and mental illness—is to validate nihilism and to let reason dissolve into irrationalism. To march toward this grim definition of freedom severs the societal thread, the human passion to "only connect," and that passion's inherent obligations toward those we love.

· · ·

$\mathcal{P}$ASSING A local deli near New York University one day, I noticed a stack of student newspapers that featured a front-page story about how fewer than 50 percent of its female undergraduates thought of themselves as feminists. I was intrigued, and curious to hear the thoughts of today's young women in that protected ivory tower space. So I sent an e-mail explaining my interest in feminism to students in an independent studies program and the journalism school.

What struck me most meeting the undergraduates who replied to my query—besides the fact that no one had ever heard of Jeane Kirkpatrick—was how much Virginia Woolf's prediction had held true. For college students who have not yet been exposed to the inequities of the marketplace, a feminism that solely champions the rights of women (once the right to earn a living has been won), and now focuses almost exclusively on the issues of dominance, pornography, and gender identity constructions, becomes for the majority of young women a dead word.

"I never had to define myself as a feminist because no one ever says that," Annelle, a college junior from North Carolina, told me. "It's not really a concept in which people are talking," she added. "But what I read, or heard, was that the movement got to a point where the people involved in it weren't willing to listen to others. They had their beliefs and they saw the world their way, which in many ways was based on reality, but then they couldn't really move on from there and got attached to this oppression."

"When I got your e-mail," Rachel, a sophomore, told me, "I thought, Feminism—would I have anything to say about feminism? But I've had a couple days to think about it."

Apparently those days didn't help. Rachel told me that although she hoped to have "some sort of feminist viewpoint of the world," for her generation feminism's message felt neither political nor current. Rachel was not apolitical, but she preferred to dedicate her spare time to global issues, attending rallies on the violence in Darfur and world poverty, and buying only fair-trade coffee, which prevented her from drinking anything at the Starbucks in which we met. She described her impatience in taking a gender studies class: "Our teacher was a feminist and she kept talking about how gender is constructed. And we were like, 'Okay, but can't we talk about something that's more relevant—like transgender?'"

The day after I met Rachel, she sent me this e-mail: "I was thinking about our meeting, and what has been bothering me was the question about the definition of feminism. You asked me what it meant, or what I thought it meant, and I gave you an answer because I really felt like I ought to have one. But I've been thinking about it, and the fact is that I've no idea what feminism means. I just have no idea."

And who could blame Rachel for being confused? In the past forty years, feminism has become a cultural palimpsest, with each new addition inviting its own revision. With the publication of *The Feminist Mystique* in 1963, Betty Friedan helped usher in "second wave" feminism (the "first wave" was begun by the suffragettes). The Enlightenment principles of personal autonomy, progress, and equality inspired this vision—which also came to be known as "liberal feminism"—and the movement in turn made a bold leap and placed its faith in the public, not private, world, urging women to wholeheartedly join in.

But African-American feminist and social activist bell hooks, along with others such as Gloria Anzaldúa and Audre Lorde, would subsequently argue that Friedan's admonition to get women out of the house dismally failed to understand the lives of women of color and the working class. Their work helped create a "third wave," which addressed "second-wave" feminism's shortcomings in the areas of race, class, ethnicity, and religion.

Yet three waves barely make a ripple in an ocean of oppression. Feminism has taken on many names and forms, including "equality feminism," "radical feminism," "difference feminism," "individualist feminism," and the environmentally friendly "ecofeminism." In the Eighties, Catherine MacKinnon focused her work on the eroticization of male dominance and female submission, and she and Andrea Dworkin became known as "anti-pornography feminists." Ellen Willis and others who challenged MacKinnon's position called themselves

"sex-positive feminists." In France, Julia Kristeva and Luce Irigaray wrote about language, desire, and body; Elaine Show-
alter labeled their work the "feminist theorization of female/
sexuality/textuality." And don't forget the influences of Marx-
ism, postmodernism, poststructuralism, psychoanalytic, and
Queer Theory on feminist thought.

Meanwhile, Britney Spears looked fat on the MTV awards.

Contemporary American feminism has primarily come to
mean championing women's autonomy and challenging the
privileging of male over female. So although Jeane Kirkpatrick
couldn't make it into the *Handbook of American Women's History*, many of the undergraduates I met believed that Condoleezza Rice is a feminist. Rice was described by young women,
who added that they were against the war, as "admirable as a
heroine of feminism," "a role model because of her high rank,"
"someone who holds a strong position in the government and
doesn't care what people say," and "breaking traditional female
roles because she's a black woman."

•   •   •

SOME YOUNG WOMEN shared my preoccupation with
reconciling the competing values of our ancestral pasts and
contemporary culture, and hoped that family traditions could
help shape a future path for them as wives and mothers. Hannahbah, a twenty-year-old Native American from New Mexico
who was double-majoring in journalism and gender/sexual-
ity studies, said she considers herself a feminist because she
shares the belief that "there is something wrong with the way

society constructs men and women's identities." Yet Hannah-bah looks to her Navajo ancestry, not mainstream feminism, to help guide her.

"Typically in my culture, women are the ones who nurture and this gives them more agency to be in charge because the domestic is seen as what's more important in life. You know, the men go out and hunt and that's not seen as contributing as much to society. It's all family-based, community-based, everyone contributes, and women are seen as the head."

"There's a joke in the Navajo community," Hannahbah added, about her matriarchal tribe's reputation: "Lakota men walk beside their women, Mohawk men walk in front of their women, but Navajo men walk behind their women."

Emi, a senior who also considers herself a feminist, explained that "the term alienates a lot of people," especially the women she knows from her working-class background, because it assumes a certain sameness. While the feminist movement was working to get women out of the home, Emi grew up around people struggling to pay the monthly bills and wanting to spend more time with their families. Emi's Japanese mother and American father had split up when she was four and they were living in Japan. Her father brought Emi to Pennsylvania while her mother remained in Japan, and Emi grew up a latchkey child taking care of herself after school while her father struggled to hold a series of jobs, from bus driver to chimney sweep.

Both Emi and Hannahbah were passionate about the thought of having children. Emi originally attended Berkeley but dropped out to work because of high tuition costs, although she then received generous scholarship offers from

Columbia and New York University. Now twenty-five, Emi told me that she recently went through a "conceptual pregnancy." She found herself preoccupied watching mothers pushing baby strollers and young children playing; indeed, the idea of giving birth held such power in her imagination that her period stopped for three months and her breasts swelled. (Her story made me wonder whether she had inherited the Japanese sensitivity to respond physiologically to intense emotional experiences. For example, the fairly common state of *kanashibari*—a condition virtually unknown in America and for which there is no word in English—afflicts victims of emotional stress, creating a temporary body paralysis.)

Deeply introspective, perhaps as a result of the many hours she spent alone as a little girl, Emi questioned, however, whether she could raise a child in today's dangerous and environmentally unstable world. Even if she did find a partner and become a mother, Emi said she'd have "a lot of doubts about hiring someone to take care of my child," concerned as she is about "the power dynamic that it creates to do such intimate work as well as the politics of who ends up doing this work." If she could reconcile both of these issues, Emi explained, "maybe I wouldn't be opposed."

Hannahbah, a middle child brought up by her father and the Navajo community after her mother died when she was five, felt certain that she would raise a child herself. Imagining her life in phases, she planned on becoming a journalist, then, after having a family, switching to the more time-manageable career of a teacher. She hoped that during the early child-rearing years, her future husband would be able to financially support their family.

"I want to be a mother who stays at home," said Han-nahbah. "And I want at that point for it to be *revered*"—she emphasized the word with a nervous and proud laugh that recalled her ancestry—"and okay in society because I feel I will be contributing greatly to society. I don't know if we'll be at that point. But that's what I want."

Listening to Hannahbah express her ideas about mother-hood, I had to double-check what I had previously jotted down because, quite frankly, her words weren't what I expected to hear from a gender and sexuality studies major. But my disbe-lief probably stemmed from memories of my own foray into gender studies in graduate school at NYU and the many nights and weekends in which I tried to read French feminists decon-structing gender through linguistic theory. Their words—or what I could comprehend from these dense texts—inspired thoughts not about motherhood—at this point the farthest thing from my mind—but anger against a patriarchal, phal-locentric society.

Hannahbah hopes to incorporate the traditions of her Native American ancestry, which treasures the act of care, into her life choices. She's not connecting with a feminism that promotes equality and autonomy without attending to the fundamental relationship of mother and child. She raised, for example, the issue of welfare reform legislation, a policy she fears could hurt Native Americans. Agreeing with welfare reform opponents, she believes that poor mothers shouldn't be forced to work. "They should be paid for the child care they do because that's contributing to society. I think that's valid and correct. But I don't see feminism pushing to get that done."

This tension between one's ancestral values and feminist

values—affecting the descendants of the New World's first members as well as the granddaughters of Old World people—reasserted itself among a number of young women with whom I met. Juliet, whose parents were born in Italy, wants more than anything, she told me, to find a balance between her "dream job" of working in public relations in New York City for an established Italian firm and raising a family with an Italian man. But she fears that this may be impossible.

No woman in her large extended Italian-American family has held a demanding full-time job along with raising children. (Her mom worked full-time when Juliet was young while her grandmother, who lived downstairs, took care of her, but Juliet's mother quit her job after having a second child.) Juliet's "American" friends "can pick up and leave," she says, but she feels greatly conflicted about permanently settling away from her family.

"I'm not saying I have it rough, but major decisions become family decisions. Getting married, although it's my decision, is ultimately going to be a family decision," explained Juliet, who doesn't think she could live in a city far from her family if they adamantly opposed the idea. "You know growing up that you're so connected to these four, five, two hundred people," she said with a laugh, referring to her huge Pennsylvania clan.

Katie-Nicole, an Italian-American who studied in Florence last year and spent the summer in the south of Italy with her Calabrian boyfriend, said she admired the strong emphasis on family that is found in Italian culture. In Calabria, she and her boyfriend had to appear at his parents' home at 2 p.m. sharp each day to share the family meal. "Every day, an hour and a half with the family. We couldn't ever break this rule.

And what was interesting too was that the mother never got a break."

After graduating from NYU, Katie-Nicole plans to live with her boyfriend in Rome before deciding on which side of the Atlantic she'll reside. But for now, she prefers the values of Italian life that she absorbed that year. "Not to say that family isn't important here, but I sometimes think work takes its place. While over there they value the original things—where we came from—we have lost focus here, being so wrapped up in the technological world."

Asked whether she considered herself a feminist, Katie-Nicole responded, "Yes and no. Yes, because I believe that women are strong and capable and intellectual beings but no because I agree with the notion that women are emotional, nurturing, domestic beings, so I guess that would go against traditional feminist thought." Katie-Nicole's role model is her own mother, who worked as a school speech pathologist when she was growing up and balanced "being the traditional female figure of the nurturer, the mother, and the wife, while being an intellectual woman."

All of the young women I met possessed the extraordinary idealism that goes hand in hand with college years. Many held onto the notion that life could be divided into phases, with one's identity easily merging into different roles without tension, doubt, or regret.

Florentina, the daughter of a British father and an Italian mother, who lived in England for much of her childhood, explained that she wanted to have a deeply fulfilling career (to save the world, as she jokingly put it), then temporarily stop working when she had children, staying home until they were five or six. "That's very important to me. My mom did that and I'm happy with the way I turned out."

It's unrealistic, of course, to expect someone at twenty to know how she'll feel ten to fifteen years from now. Yet the assuredness that a young woman like Florentina possessed, the notion that she could easily switch from one role to the other, brought back memories of the confusion I felt after my son was born, fifteen years after I had left graduate school. It was only then that I discovered the extraordinary demands of attending to a baby, and how providing this care, especially for a woman who lacks the help and involvement of a larger, supportive community, was a lot more isolating and difficult than I had previously imagined.

Listening to the ideas and plans of these women, I felt frustrated that I couldn't convey how hard it is to give up the freedoms they now take for granted, along with the intellectual life they pursue; how the autonomy they experience in college is unique and irreplaceable; how few good jobs exist outside of independent work that allow women to leave the workforce for many years and then return; and how much political work needs to be done to challenge the reality of today's marketplace to better protect the interests of women. I wondered whether, if their generation was presented with real choices—ones in which they could reduce their working hours without fear of repercussions or marginalization—they would choose to combine work and motherhood rather than waiting for years to return to the workforce. Many of these young women already seemed poised to drop out of the marketplace before ever entering it, and they believed they could do so without significant financial repercussions.

Of all the women I met, only Annelle was certain that she didn't want to have children. Her response surprised me because she described herself as being part of a close family in which her physician mother managed to accomplish "what she really wanted to do in life—which was to have a great career, two children, and a loving husband." Annelle, whose father is also a doctor, was cared for by babysitters as a child and felt "fairly autonomous because mom was at work so I did things myself." When I suggested that she had a successful role model before her, Annelle responded, "I don't want to have kids. My brother could have kids. . . . I just don't want to be tied down. . . . In that sense, autonomy is very important for me."

Annelle's certainty about not having children could change as rapidly as Florentina's wish to stay home until her children are five or six. It wasn't these future dreams that intrigued me, but simply hearing their thoughtful, myriad voices, all of which reminded me how a woman's identity is rooted not only in generational values but in her ancestral and family background.

Surely, interviews with the dozen young women I met was far from a scientific survey, but the repeated themes that emerged in these conversations struck me deeply. My e-mail specified that I wanted to talk about the meaning of feminism and ask each woman whether she considered herself a feminist. I wondered whether the nature of my inquiry might have skewed the answers by attracting more activist students.

But what I didn't realize, viewing the world from the perspective of my own school days, was that feminism's ashes had long ago fluttered above the trees and the arch of this new generation's campus. For college students such as Gabriela, the daughter of Romanian immigrants, the first time the word "feminist" entered her lexicon was in tenth grade when she was studying *Anna Karenina*. The teacher asked her English class at Stuyvesant, a public high school for New York's highest-performing students, whether they thought of themselves as feminists. Gabriela said that only one "punked out girl" with multiple body piercings and dyed hair raised her hand.

"I was not like her. I thought I must not be one." Gabriela, who is pre-med, says that only now has she become more aware of the issues that concern women, especially women in science, as well as her need to contribute to society rather than "just staying home or acting in preconstructed notions of what it means to be a woman." She finds that her friends studying the liberal arts often don't share her views. To her disappointment, some have even mocked other young women who formed social justice groups. "I'm in science so I know there's a great difference between how men and women are treated. A lot of girls studying French, English, and music are in fields where people expect them to be, so maybe they don't experience the same kinds of prejudices."

To many of these young women, my questions about feminism and autonomy seemed downright quaint. Why would someone going to school in New York City and living on her own in the twenty-first century think a lot about the problem of achieving personal autonomy? When I recalled the article from their student newspaper—that slightly below 50 percent of female undergraduates called themselves feminists, a surprisingly low number to me—they all responded that the figure was much higher than they would have imagined, and that their liberal campus was not representative of the rest of the country.

At times when our discussions turned personal, I felt maternal toward them, wanting to grab their hands and say that life runs differently than our plans. I wanted to tell them that we'll never really know what needs to be known about life all at once; its truths are imparted slowly over time. But how didactic and depressing that would have sounded. Who better embodies limitless possibilities and the potential for change than a twenty year old? To be robbed of those first promises and thrills, left only with the weight of experience, would be to begin our tales like the wizened old Wife of Bath sharing her gap-toothed wisdom five husbands later.

A Voice of One's Own

*I*N COLLEGE and graduate school, I, too, eagerly mapped out my future plans, and yearned to apply the gender theories that I had read in the secluded comfort of the library to the world outside. And soon enough, I walked into the most famous alternative newspaper in the country, joining the very symbol of "*La Vie Boheme*," as the characters in the musical *Rent* commemorated my first office in song. Looking back to the Eighties, they raised their glasses in a toast to choice—and "To the *Village Voice*."

I was set to toss my red beret into the air and make it on my own in New York City. I even had my own apartment, a large airy studio shared with a Japanese journalist named Yoko, who left Tokyo and her husband for a year to study drama on a scholarship. She was one of those miraculous roommates—kind, attentive, and a great cook who made me sushi for dinner while I was earning a master's degree in English and working as an intern at the *Voice*. Doing as I pleased during the day with Yoko preparing a delicious Japanese meal each night, I understood firsthand why every man wants a wife.

Meanwhile, the *Village Voice* nurtured—in writer Ellen Willis's words—a feminism that "captured the rawness of our urge to transcend limits." The feminists deconstructed gender, defended pornography as free speech, and passionately ran the cultural sections of the paper. Unfortunately, I barely participated in this dialogue because I covered local news with the male political reporters, and was busy trying to find a place for myself among men enamored with a mythology from which I had spent years trying to distance myself—the machismo of the mobster.

You didn't need to be particularly astute to figure out rather quickly that, despite its nostalgic remembrance in *Rent*, the office was far from a bohemian paradise. During my time there, the relationship between the front-of-the-book news-men and the back-of-the-book cultural editors deteriorated from a wary tolerance to downright mudslinging. The women editors dubbed my male colleagues the "white boys"—in response, they asserted, to being called "Stalinest feminists." The reason for this deterioration was complicated and years in the making. But it eventually erupted, I believe, over the very issue of female autonomy.

The office I worked in no longer exists, the building torn down in a redevelopment project and replaced by a cineplex with giant screens and comfy stadium seating. The movie theater is a fitting tribute to a place where dramas exploded weekly—"You talkin' to me?"—as a script unfolded that seemed part Scorcese, part Truffaut, and where people revealed far more about their personal lives than you really needed to know. Never did I imagine on that crisp September morning when I entered the building at 842 Broadway to plead for an internship that I would spend the rest of the Eighties in these grungy, mice-infested, exasperating, and exhilarating offices, partaking in, or just leaning back to relax and enjoy, the show.

•   •   •

"ℰXPECT THE UNEXPECTED," the *Voice* motto greeted me in a framed poster as I walked—for the first time—down the main corridor past advertising and art to the editorial department. Reporters and editors were circulating near the desk of editorial receptionist Marilyn Savino, pulling off pink message slips tacked to a large bulletin board that hung on the wall. Marilyn led me to the cluttered office of Wayne Barrett, one of the *Voice*'s top investigative journalists, who at the time happened to need another intern. With coincidence in my favor, he looked at my meager portfolio of college newspaper clippings and said he'd give me a try.

"Do you think it was my résumé?" I asked Marilyn a few weeks later, during one of our routine chats always interrupted by ringing phones and the refrain: "Editorial, can I help you?"

"He thinks you're cute," Marilyn replied, inhaling her cigarette before answering the next call. Marilyn's compassionate face and gossip-loving nature made her a great listener and talker. For many of us, she doubled as office mom; she was a marvelous *mamma del sud*, worried about our sniffles and how we were getting along while sharing her grilled veggies drizzled with olive oil.

Although my knowledge of local politics was limited to what I read in the Metro section of the *New York Times*, I was eager to learn, and Wayne brought me to a file cabinet filled with copies of his "NYC" column, which he co-wrote each week with colleague Joe Conason. I jumped at the chance to show off my critical reading abilities and pored through pages of worn newspaper clippings with a pen and notebook in hand. But soon I developed a sinking feeling. Awash in county leaders, district school boards, poverty barons, greedy lobbyists, and needy politicians, the world of city politics and its inevitable corruption—distilled into the bare-bones fact of who has made an offer one can't refuse—eluded me.

Reading just a few issues of the *Voice*'s densely packed "NYC" section quickly pushed me overboard, and I was drowning in the names of literally hundreds of political players. A typical paragraph in one of Wayne's columns read: "[Ted] Teah was appointed to an eight-year term on the [planning] commission by Beame in 1977, though his prior planning experience was limited to the legal assistance he'd given to poverty baron Ramon Velez in stripmining the South Bronx. Teah's rise to prominence of a Cohn partnership is strictly political. He's gone from working in a Velez employment program to serving as an associate for Velez's longtime counsel Paul Bleifer to joining the firm of Paul Victor, counsel to the Bronx Democratic organization." A subsequent column included this addition: "Teah's wife, Ann Baldau, is a $29,000-a-year special assistant to Board of Education member Robert Christen. Like Teah, Christen has his own ties to the Bronx organization, including a daughter who was a consultant in the recent campaign of Bronx Borough President Stanley Simon."

Every name carried meaning and weight, signs and signifiers in a field of corruption and greed, and I was left to parse the role played by clubhouses, law firms, developers, county organizations, and assorted others in influence peddling. Practically all the players were men, and even the news stories tightly packed on the page—couldn't they have added some attractive graphics?—felt as claustrophobic as a windowless basement club. Wayne was initially impressed with my diligence in reading his work, but he soon realized that although I pretended to absorb much ink, my mind held about a paper towel's worth.

Wayne's other intern, a leftist lesbian who eyed me suspiciously, thinking that she had regrettably been paired with "Gidget Goes to the *Voice*" (her words), was fearless when I was timid. She could detect my trepidation reporting in crime-ridden neighborhoods. We may never have become close if not for a defining moment a few months into our internships. I walked up to her, frustrated and angry with a reporter I had tried to work with that day, and blurted out that he was a misogynist. She smiled broadly, and a friendship grew.

More than a decade after I left the *Voice*, the writer Bill Tonelli described in a humorous essay for the *New York Times* why men were fascinated with the television series *The Sopranos*. His witty observations about machismo felt like time bottled from my *Voice* days. Mobsters do, Tonelli wrote, "what most men, in their hearts, wish they could do: spend time with one another out and about, idle and unrestrained by the civilizing presence of women in their workplace, free to drink, smoke, curse, eat thick sandwiches of meat and cheese and carry guns and fat rolls of large-denomination bills."

On Tuesday afternoons, after the previous night's late deadline, the political writers would leisurely meet for thick sandwiches of meat and cheese and discuss the next week's story ideas at Bradley's, a smoky jazz bar that once stood in the Central Village. I occasionally received the perk of an invitation to Bradley's, although I always felt like the tagalong younger sister (to be treated with respect) who smiled and listened while sipping a Tab with lemon.

"I'm thinking about buying a piece," a reporter told me in a hushed voice, taking a drag on his cigarette as we sat in his small cubicle.

"A what?" I replied, clueless.

"A piece. The reporting I'm doing is getting more dangerous. It's time to get a gun."

A features editor required copy with "edge," called women "chicks," and kept a bottle of scotch in his desk. At the end of the day, he would invite favorite male writers to his dimly lit office, and they'd raise their feet and sip Johnny Walker Black.

No one, however, carried fat rolls of large-denomination bills.

At this hip downtown newspaper, the voice of Jeane Kirkpatrick rang in my ears. "Politics is, in a certain sense, a competitive sport," she once told me. "At the level that it is engaged in as politics rather than public policy, it is a competitive sport. In most societies and in most of history, competitive sports have been dominated by males rather than females."

I had written a *Voice* feature that asked whether a conservative woman could be a feminist. But perhaps first I should have inverted the question: Can a liberal man be a sexist?

Why, yes, Mr. Grant. Why did I even bother to ask?

.   .   .

*T*HE DISTINCTION BETWEEN politics and public policy matched the click of my typewriter keys. The political game didn't much interest me, but once I shifted my attention to policy issues, particularly the city's lack of affordable housing, the landscape of New York, partitioned into parcels of rich and poor, privileged and vulnerable, powerful and exploited, filled my once sparse notebook. As a twenty-two year old, I had the opportunity to write my first article, which I hoped would expose the cruelties of an exploding housing market and a city tax abatement policy that encouraged the swift rehabilitation of cheap rooming hotels into luxury apartments. Seemingly overnight, musty hotels had become opulent quarters. Unceremoniously, elderly and unstable former residents had been thrown out of their homes. One old man even lost his false teeth when hired goons dumped his possessions down the exit staircase. In these Manhattan-style conversions, gilt replaced grime, and toothless old men were forced into what was left of a dwindling housing supply or, for some, homeless shelters and the streets.

In E. B. White's words, I became one of the city's "worshipful beginners," coming to New York hoping to make a difference as a reporter and finding my "own brand of tonic to stay alive." Wayne was a superb teacher, and he and Joe passed along invaluable story ideas and tips. Injustice had fueled my world-view since childhood, and now I was empowered by a reader-ship that could share my outrage. I eagerly scoured the streets of newly gentrified Manhattan looking for former hotel residents who had become homeless. With a little luck, I found a few, although telling their stories was a job handed to the men.

Articles that appeared in "NYC" needed to sound like the column's writers, and the occasional contributor received a byline only after the story had been "run through the typewriter" by Wayne or Joe. Running it through the typewriter—literally, in a pre-computer age—meant anything from a complete rewrite to spicing up the language with choice phrases like "the mayor and his minions" or "the fat man of the South Bronx." Because I wanted to get my work into print, I grudg-ingly accepted this other voice inhabiting my story.

Eventually I concluded that to advance my career, I would have to imitate the language of men. The mayor would have his minions, the city council leader his sorry sycophants; and I too would berate the fat man of the South Bronx. After a year as an intern, I wanted nothing more than to settle in perma-nently. I had found a home, albeit a highly dysfunctional one, but that was the only kind I knew.

We gathered around the editorial desk to collect messages, gossip, and reaffirm our otherness as members of this Green-wich Village weekly. Or as the singers from *Rent* declared in their celebration of *"La Vie Boheme"*: "To starving for attention / Hating convention, hating pretension. / To being an us for once . . . instead of a them!"

"That bitch," huffed an editor, reading the name of a writer off her message slip as she passed several boy reporters staging a water pistol fight around the editorial desk. The mostly girl copy department, on the other side of the floor, debated at length whether the phrase "blow job" should be hyphenated. The vote was no as a noun and yes as an adjective—that is, the blow-job president, presciently establishing a style guideline a decade before Monica Lewinsky. Writers slugged out their differences with one another in print—and occasionally in person—and announced unabridged intimate details of their lives.

"We have to fuck tonight," a writer explained to an editor as to why he couldn't meet the next day's deadline. The writer's wife was on a fertility drug regimen.

This purposeful testing of limits by poking at boundaries, peeing in public, flipped the experience of my childhood, in which my family struggled to fit in but looked more like *The Munsters*. To grow up in suburbia with a brother who speaks in confused sentences that start in the middle of a thought, then loop to the beginning and sometimes manage to find a muddled end, who sits silently in a dark corner of the den where your friends have come to play, goads one to rant against conformity. "Banality, mediocrity, superficiality," I'd mutter as a teenager, nodding at the Dead End sign that signaled the truth about our street, rejecting the comfort of dinner aromas that seeped out front doors as the commuter train from New York City whistled in.

My family was intensely self-conscious about how others perceived us. They were wounded by the continual bruises of public engagements—the embarrassed, irritated glance of the listener who wanted my brother to stop talking; the disapproving nod of the church parishioner toward my brother as he offered a nonstop handshake. So for me, it was cathartic to watch Voicers intentionally take on the role of the elephant in the room.

. . .

*T*HE EMOTIONAL CENTER of the department, the editorial desk, eventually changed hands when Marilyn was promoted to secretary to the editor in chief, and another employee, Jesus (which he pronounced the biblical way) Diaz was asked to field phone calls.

"Maria, here's a message for you. Can you believe this guy's name is Moses?" he said in earnest, waving the pink paper as I grabbed the number of a housing organizer I'd been trying to reach.

"Thank you, Jesus."

The *Voice* had some of the weirdness of a religious revival meeting, all passion and unstoppable tongues housed together under one roof. The intense fervor, however, was not focused on a single entity but depended upon the section of the paper for which you wrote. The biggest *Voice* chasm during my tenure existed between the boys and the girls—that is, the front-of-the-book newsmen and the back-of-the-book cultural editors.

The reporters took charge of politics; the feminists—who, like the men, had mostly come of age in the consciousness-raising Sixties—edited much of the cultural writing. This setup exemplified a newspaper's usual gender divide between those who cover the "hard" and the "soft" news. If the boys looked to southern Italy for a model of the *capo di tutti capi*, the girls preferred the *je ne sais quoi* of neighboring France and its burgeoning movement of feminist cultural theory. As the name-calling went into full gear and relationships disintegrated, the "Stalinest feminists" and the "white boys" shared much animosity and also some strange prose, like the moment of self-revelation in a book review in which a writer declared "color me a balding white boy."

Color me a dark-haired white girl; I was never included in the back-of-the-book by the feminists. They viewed me as a local reporter, not a cultural critic like themselves. And at a newspaper that rewards quirky individualism, one rarely finds a collective community ethos—or a divine Ya-Ya sisterhood. Daily life at the *Voice*, for all its talk of inclusion, was hierarchical (what mattered was whether you were part of the men's or women's hierarchy) and so highly individualistic that even the essential tools of the trade couldn't be passed around or borrowed. This sentiment was best summed up by a feminist writer who stopped by the office about once a week. When she walked in unexpectedly one day and saw me using the typewriter at her desk, I swallowed hard.

"Typewriters are like toothbrushes," she told me. "They can't be shared."

. . .

*A*s IN MOST UNHAPPY families, difficulties brew and simmer for years until a particular incident brings down the house. Like a battle that erupts in the kitchen during a tense holiday, the *Voice* fight centered on yams. A feature by writer C. Carr about the downtown performance artist Karen Finley became the week's cover story, and Carr described how in one of her boundary-breaking acts Finley pulled down her pants and stuffed yams in her ass. Pete Hamill, who was then writing for the *Voice*, read the article that morning and promptly rounded up the front-of-the-book men to march into the editor-in-chief's office. Yes, they had to put up with the *Voice*'s famous personal ads seeking attractive gay men in leather, but how, they demanded to know, could such a disgusting story be featured so prominently on the cover of *their* newspaper? Who would ever take them seriously again?

But Finley's whole purpose was to rage and outrage. She decried women's continued mistreatment in a male-dominated society that eroticized control through acts of domestic violence, and she channeled her volcanic anger into a performance that shattered acceptable boundaries. The apoplectic political writers, however, focused on a singular question: Were the yams raw or cooked?

For the back-of-the-book editors, Carr wrote just the kind of piece they wanted: If women sought freedom from patriarchy through autonomy, then who more than Finley expressed the most brazen form of self? Carr concluded her analysis of Finley's performance by invoking the language and ideas of French feminist theorists. These feminists, influenced by structural anthropologist Claude Lévi-Strauss and psychoanalyst Jacques Lacan, wanted to debunk the symbolic image of the all-powerful phallus that denigrates women: "What I desire and what I am waiting for," wrote Luce Irigaray, "is what men will do and say if their sexuality gets loose from the empire of phallocratism."

To the French feminists, the very structure of language was "phallocentric"—that is, it privileged the phallus by associating masculinity with more potent images (intelligence versus sensitivity, head versus heart) than the weaker femininity, and they wanted to challenge this hierarchical linguistic power, make it go limp. Carr argued that when Finley described sex and rage as the same impulse, as in her stories of forced anal sex, domestic violence, and a child abuser named Mr. Horse, she knocked "the self-censor down" and told on "Mr. Horse, her father, the culture." Carr concluded that because Finley was debunking masculine domination through language and boundary-breaking storytelling, "gender difference based on possession or lack of a dick has disappeared."

The furious overreaction of the front-of-the-book men, the *Voice* feminists concluded, only further confirmed their prudishness and philistinism, unaware as they were of structuralism, semiotics, and the French deconstruction movement. Ah, the women could sigh, the white boys: They comfortably resided in their narrow little black-and-white world in which the theories of Lévi-Strauss came down to prewashed and husky size.

But the political writers saw a diminished interest in and, in practical terms, less newspaper space devoted to what were once the passions of their age. As Pete Hamill had asked in *The Sense of the Sixties*, an essay anthology assigned to my brother Bob in college and which I clutched as a ten year old wanting to imitate him: "How do you tell your children what it was like to be alive when John Kennedy was a man and not an airport?"

These men were proponents of a Kennedy-style liberalism. They talked about yesterday's Goodman, Cheney, and Schwerner and today's continued segregation of blacks from the white power structure. To them, government had a duty to redirect its resources to the poorest members of society, and they were going to expose the corruption and greed that stymied such progress—from the incompetent bureaucrat to antipoverty programs gone bad. Hamill complained publicly that the week the Finley article ran, the *Voice* had failed to cover "the largest antiapartheid rally in the city's history."

Like those critics of autonomy whom philosopher Kwame Anthony Appiah sharply described two decades later in his book *The Ethics of Identity*, the men were angered by the "arrogant insularity" of the language of autonomy: "All that talk of self-fashioning, self-direction, self-authorship suggests a bid to create the Performance Art Republic, elbowing aside Grandma Walton in order to make the world safe for Karen Finley."

The men had interpreted the Finley article as a dangerous threat to their beliefs about men and women, religion and secularism, traditionalism and modernism. And like most threatened people, the men had convinced themselves that the values upon which they were raised had been attacked and scorned: "In the *Voice*," wrote Hamill in a scathing column about the Finley piece, "it's always acceptable to make vile remarks about Catholics, but never, ever under any conceivable circumstances, about gays."

Years later, Finley wondered in a memoir how the liberal *Village Voice* and civil rights advocate Pete Hamill ended up attacking her work as viciously as Jesse Helms had launched his own tirade against Finley. Helms, the Republican senator from North Carolina, who supported apartheid in South Africa; sang "Dixie" to Carol Moseley-Braun after she was

elected the first African-American woman senator; and ran a
campaign commercial that zoomed in on a white hand crum-
bling an application while a voice-over commented: "You
needed that job . . . but they had to give it to a minority."
Despite the political writers' left-wing credentials, when the
subject matter turned to aggressive female sexuality, these
men responded just like their foes on the right.

The response to the Finley article and the internally
debated question of the *Voice*'s identity in the Eighties and
Nineties mirrored the open wound left in the Democratic
Party from the 1972 Nixon-McGovern election, when the
Johnson-Humphrey wing separated from the McGovern left
and pitted proponents of the Great Society against those who
wanted bolder cultural change. In classic liberal tradition, the
larger agenda for social reform was lost because of internal
squabbles, and the *Voice*'s alternative politics ended up in as
lonely a place as George McGovern accepting his party's nom-
ination at two o'clock in the morning before a public that had
long gone to bed.

*   *   *

$\mathcal{D}$ESPITE THE political writers' incorrigibly male behavior,
including Wayne's delight in sexist self-parody, slapping his
thigh to suggest the perfect seat for his female interns, I disagreed with the feminists eager to write off the men because
they didn't share their vision of progressivism. Putting aside
his occasional fits of anger coupled with an imposing physical
height that made me cower as he roared, Wayne discerned the
poet's test of what women want. He offered me an unmatched

generosity. Taking a leave to work on a book, Wayne suggested that I write the "NYC" column in his absence. At the time I was a copy editor waiting for the opening of a full-time writing job. Then editor-in-chief David Schneiderman, who was equally supportive, agreed.

My first article to lead the column page advocated that the city employ a system of wage parity between men and women workers known as comparable worth. Appropriately headlined "Girls Just Wanna Have Parity," the only typewriter that the article ran through was my own. For a few months, I decided the tone and content of "NYC" because, in an act of respect for my work, Wayne offered me sovereignty—a sovereignty over self, not over others. And in that brief period of time, Marina Warner's utopian definition rang true: Through negotiated exchanges of generosity and trust, my emancipation from former intern to columnist came from a man's increasing understanding.

But life, as we know, is not a fairy tale. Eventually the knight returned from his publishing joust to take back his column. Another two years passed before I was hired as a staff writer, during which I was an impatient lady-in-waiting at the copy desk, grumbling about an exhausting twelve-hour shift that sent me to Hackensack, New Jersey, every Monday night to proofread newspaper galleys until five in the morning.

The thrill of working for a newspaper despite earning low wages, or none as an intern, was also wearing thin. "If they'd only pay me what they get paid for one of those futon ads," Warren Leight, a freelance humorist who became a Tony-award-winning playwright, once remarked to me about the *Voice*'s legendary cheapness. I agreed, and made sure not to spend all at once the fifteen-dollar bonus I found in my pay-check that Christmas.

By the time I left the *Voice*, my optimism had begun to fade; my own brand of tonic had fizzled out. After spending nearly a decade writing about the homeless, the mentally ill homeless, the poorly treated illegal immigrants, the prisoners with AIDS, the senior citizens evicted from their residences, the mentally retarded people drugged and abused in institutions, and many of life's other miserable victims, I was a little depressed. The social problems on which I reported were intractable, the improvements minuscule. Two decades later, the same stories repeat, as does the same lack of political will and money to solve them.

I was also harangued by a new editor in chief who showed me a particular type of animosity, far harsher in his criticism of women than of men: "There's not a paragraph, a sentence, or a kernel of thought in your article that's worth printing."

Not even a subordinate clause?

I found myself at a point that I think all journalists reach at least once in their career, whether having had a story killed for political reasons; being passed over for someone with more style and less substance; witnessing the rise of a reporter who makes up wholesale fictions with a con man's confident swagger; watching a politician's promises disappear at the whiff of an approaching reelection; learning that ad revenue sings louder than copy; fearing the exploitation of the vulnerable under the guise of telling their story; or simply growing bored with a news article's formulaic approach that must ignore life's myriad textures. When I reached that point and considered that days, weeks, or months of work were routinely tossed into the garbage like fish wrapping, I thought about the gray-stubbled face of my great-uncle Patsy sitting sullenly in his chair like an old seaman who once navigated turbulent waters but has forgotten where his ship is docked.

Yes, you were right, Uncle Patsy, I heard myself saying: Everything is bullshit.

* * *

I LEFT THE *Voice* to become the chief speechwriter to David N. Dinkins, New York's first African-American mayor, who hired a diverse group of men and women to work in his administration. The top city hall positions of deputy mayors were initially occupied by three men and two women, and I had enthusiastically covered the inclusiveness of the Dinkins administration in a political column I was writing for the *Voice*. Perhaps a little too enthusiastically. Six months into the new administration, the mayor's press secretary invited me to lunch and asked whether I wanted the speechwriting job.

As I should have expected, most of the major political decisions ended up being made by men, but still it was refreshing to hear the voice of a woman deputy mayor discussing policy options on the phone while trying to calm the cries of her children. The cadence of "mommy, mommy" pulsed stronger than any line I could craft about structural budget deficits and economic redevelopment ("more money, more money"?). Yet that deputy mayor left midterm because the rigorous demands of the job and its exhausting schedule took too high a toll on her family life.

I now knew that navigating the internecine plots that accompany any high-level position and working the requisite twelve-hour days called for more skill and stamina than the mere toss of a beret. And although I realized the silliness of believing in a Hollywood fantasy of female achievement, still I found it entertaining to meet the cultural icon who made the image famous: I volunteered to write a speech for Mary Tyler Moore when she hosted a Dinkins fund-raiser.

During my city hall days, I relived the *Voice* motto of "Expect the Unexpected," finding similarities in the experience that defined my twenties in the least anticipated places. I accompanied the mayor on trips to Europe, Asia, Africa, and the Middle East and spent time traveling in foreign cities with prominent chief executive officers from New York who were invited to explore overseas business opportunities. Just as my dad made extra money as a young man working weekends as a caddy, lugging the golf clubs of CEOs past gentle green mounds and sand traps, his daughter, as a member of the mayor's staff, would overhear the banter of these businessmen in far corners of the world.

"Can't I get a roast beef sandwich anywhere in this city?" one real estate executive complained during a traditional Japanese dinner as he stared into a porcelain bowl of miso soup crowned with shavings of eighteen-carat gold that danced like a glittery sunburst on a dark pond.

"She's so beautiful, so smart," a CEO in his sixties bragged about his new young wife. We listened to a long list of her attributes while sitting in a traffic jam in downtown Tokyo.

"And how did you manage to get her?" another man teased.

"Simple," he replied. "I have a Lear jet."

The same lust for thick sandwiches of meat and cheese. A Lear jet replacing a piece as the symbol of male power. (Will men ever break loose "from the empire of phallocratism"?) Corporate CEOs and alternative journalists; subject and reporter; capitalist proponent and socialist antagonist; loud, opinionated revelers joyfully leaving behind the civilizing presence of women. Free to be boys on the bus.

With one difference. Finally I was meeting men who carried fat rolls of large-denomination bills.

Sacrifice

THE GERANIUMS SIT in a large aluminum planter on the windowsill; their leaves pulsate like the beat of tiny hearts. The soft slap of morning air has awoken these plants of different stripes: the green-leaved young, sturdy stalks of the already bloomed, and shriveled brown petals that hang from stems like empty cocoons or garden bees humming silently. A pigeon swoops down for a breakfast snack and munches on some blushing flowered stalks. How much of the delicate plant will the pigeon destroy?

"Perhaps none of us are truly ourselves, it occurs to me, but only ourselves at a certain age. . . . We have no identity apart from our age," remarks the narrator of Tim Parks's novel *Europa*. To stare at the potted geraniums, the life cycle handed to me in a silver-colored planter, how can I not accept

Parks's observation? If I were to define myself today, no doubt I'd answer differently than when I was at the *Village Voice* twenty years before.

I began to pay more attention to how people looked at me when I was in my thirties, as the bloom of youth began to fade and important choices needed to be made. "My brother thought she was a lesbian," a relative cheerfully told my friend after my wedding reception, revealing their relief that at thirty-four I had finally found a man.

It was a December wedding, the season devoted to the Nativity, not to nuptials, the month in the old days when women said "I do" only if they *had* to. And our timing was more pragmatic than romantic. My husband, Tony (I had to break it to Mom that I had found a Jewish Tony), has devoted most of his career to public service. I had been working in government as a speechwriter, so we wished for a wedding officiated by Mayor Dinkins that celebrated those aspects of our lives.

We remained optimistic that Dinkins would win a second term (a June wedding perhaps?), but we soon realized that of votes and vows, only the former should be left to democracy. Taking the personal as political to a new extreme, we needed to act quickly before our idea of a wedding in Gracie Mansion, the mayor's residence, would be rudely annulled by the New Year's arrival of Rudy Giuliani. Tony offered a quick proposal, knee down on the cold November pavement, shortly after we had left the Sheraton hotel where Dinkins supporters had gathered to watch the election results—and ultimately the concession speech. Two days after we had made this decision to publicly sanction our private four-year union, I offered the mayor my condolences and popped him the question: "Will you marry me?"

In the months that followed, friends began to offer advice over grilled fish and steamed vegetables: "You'd make a great mom, you know." Tick. Tick. Tick. But I couldn't think about motherhood then, having grown up in a family that feared momentous change and was afraid to acknowledge the inevitable movement of life or welcome its additions. I wanted to experience first what it felt like to be part of a married couple. Besides, having grown up with a disabled sibling, I was apprehensive about having a child. I had seen the wounds inflicted from too much self-denial, from delivering continual care.

. . .

*T*HERE'S AN old parlor game about identity that supposes an alien descends from outer space to learn about the strange creatures who inhabit this place. In this close encounter of the therapeutic kind, the alien asks each person to describe himself with three nouns. When the scenario was posed to Lyndon B. Johnson, he famously declared: "I am a free man, an American, and a Democrat."

Simone de Beauvoir addressed the issue of female identity, and the shadow in which women have found themselves behind men of power and means, in her classic work, *The Second Sex*. She stated in the book's preface: "But if I wish to define myself, I must first of all say: 'I am a woman'; on this truth must be based all further discussion."

Half a century later, after the feminist movement sought to erase discrimination based on gender, does de Beauvoir's assertion remain true, that who we are must begin with "I am a woman"? It's doubtful that women would offer the same response as LBJ: "I'm a free woman" sounds more like the line of a husky-throated divorcée with a scotch in her hand than a declaration of national and individual liberty.

At the *Voice*, I would have answered "journalist" for the first noun, probably American for the second. But if I had honestly acknowledged the particular genetic, familial, and cultural blend that made me who I am, my response would have been: an Italian-American woman who grew up with a disabled sibling. The answer probably disqualifies me from the parlor game's catchier format—and my response would need to change over time because the word "mother" is now essential. This selective construction, or reconstruction, of my answer reflects, of course, the ways in which I have chosen to see the world, as well as how those choices have been influenced—and imposed upon me—by the life and family into which I was born.

Entering adulthood believing that I didn't want to have a child, I could have made a bad decision for myself, if not otherwise persuaded by a loving husband. Yet, once we did have a child, having grown up with a disabled sibling affected me in more ways than I could have imagined. For one, I hadn't become aware of, until tested by an infant, the built-in reserve of patience acquired over a lifetime of attending to a brother whose needs always remained the same. I also hadn't recognized how my mother's willingness to surrender her desires to care for my brother, a way of life brought about by circumstances outside of her control, ultimately revealed itself to me as the flip side of the American obsession with autonomy.

. . .

*C*OULD YOU hold my watch for me, pigeon?"

Pigeon, the girl bird, was the nickname that my brother Henry gave to me. It was the 1960s, when LBJ was president and suburban adolescents reveled in summer's freedom, playing leisurely games of softball after dinner around our cul-de-sac, running the bases while crickets hummed. On this evening, a rare event had taken place—the neighborhood boys had asked my brother to join them. Henry didn't have any friends on the block, but at least the Short Hills teenagers were nicer to him than the rougher-edged boys from Cranford, according to my mother, who wished to leave the working-class town as soon as my parents had moved there. In Cranford, my mother preferred that Henry stay inside after dinner because the neighborhood kids would routinely humiliate my brother with greetings like "Hey, stupid."

Henry was eager to play ball but was always fastidious about his possessions, so he asked me to hold his prized Bulova watch. Happy to be the girl cheerleader, although anxious about how my oldest brother would be accepted, I sat on the curb and leaned my back against the telephone pole dug into our front lawn. On this balmy summer evening, I listened to the clatter of wooden bats hitting the pavement and the scratch of sneakers sliding toward the curb that stood for first base. Praying that Henry could catch the tossed ball and rooting for both my brothers, I mindlessly stretched the gold-plated watchband's little accordion links in my hands—pull, press, pull, press, pull, press, pull . . .

Snap.

Could you hold my watch, pigeon? What did the pigeon destroy?

With the little gold links resting in my sweaty palms, I wished I could fly away to escape the circle of hell that I had inadvertently created with my own two hands. At eight, I was old enough to know that even minor events could have enormous consequences because my brother's mental retardation, coupled with mental illness, was a toxic combination. I knew how my brother would rage against imperfection until each nick, wound, or broken link could be repaired.

Before the game was over, I ran up the staircase, two steps at a time, to warn my parents about what I had done. My father shook his head in icy silence. "Oh my God," my mother moaned. My carelessness would make the more than fair share of daily pain she experienced caring for my brother even worse than she could imagine. I had expected their anger, but I was unprepared for the rage that this incident would unleash in my brother. When I handed Henry the tiny links of his favorite possession, his face switched from bewilderment to anger and turned red. He screamed and cursed at me like the man-child he was, out of control, flailing his arms, moving closer as my parents pulled him away.

I began my Pavlovian dash around the dining room table, the "Maria run," as my brother Bob labeled my routine response to Henry's outbursts. Never knowing how to handle my fear, I'd circle round and round, the tiny mouse scratching the treadmill to nowhere, seeking relief in mere exhaustion. Finally my father, who could stand it no longer, jumped into the car to search for any repair shop that might be open in the evening. Miraculously, he returned with a new watchband, providing a temporary calm by closing the door on this crisis. But it would be only a matter of time before the next one would emerge.

"Think about your other children." My mother used to repeat aloud the advice of those who told her it was best to put Henry in an institution for the sake of the rest of us. Thirteen years younger than my brother, I didn't know him in a gentler stage, the little boy with a patch over his lazy eye, prone to seizures and trying to navigate the larger world. Henry was born in 1946, before the era of early intervention, social workers, and consent decrees to ensure that special ed children received proper resources. I imagine that when my parents lived with my grandmother, life was easier for my family because my brother had not yet experienced adolescence and its hormonal outbursts, and he was surrounded by cousins who enjoyed playing with him. When Henry entered my consciousness, it was as an isolated teenager, and his irrational behavior caused a crazy anxiety in me.

At the time, there were no national models of compassionate care. Rather there were sinister stories about private pain, such as former president Kennedy's mentally retarded sister, who had been lobotomized decades earlier when the paterfamilias decided to permanently institutionalize his daughter to preserve the good Kennedy name. Americans had not yet been exposed to the shocking scenes inside Willowbrook, the state-supported institution for children with mental retardation in Staten Island, New York. In the Seventies, Willowbrook became a national symbol of neglect and abuse after television reporter Geraldo Rivera exposed its appalling conditions. But the response in the Sixties was to shut damage away.

I'm not sure why my mother repeated her friends' admonition, perhaps out of sorrow for what Henry put us through. The other mothers, seeing the daily hardship of my mother's life, offered advice—rational, heartfelt advice common to the thinking of that era, intended to help four out of five of us, and to give my mother the freedom to choose the extent of her sacrifice. Some told her to drug my brother until he was passive; others said to put him in an institution. But my mother could not put her own flesh and blood in a state mental hospital. My parents eventually went to a neurologist about Henry's volatile mood swings. The doctor prescribed a powerful antipsychotic drug that my brother was to take along with his phenobarbital and Dilantin, the little white pill and capsule he swallowed several times a day to prevent seizures.

But when Henry responded to the medication by sitting silently in a chair and staring blankly, my mother understood that this kind of "therapy" relieved the caregiver by hurting the dependent, and she stopped giving him the pills. (In the early Eighties, when I spent several months reporting on the abysmal conditions of a state mental institution that also housed the mentally retarded, I saw the same blank expressions on motionless people who developed tardive dyskinesia, the involuntary facial contortions, twitching, and drooling that result from the prolonged use of antipsychotic drugs.)

For decades my mother searched for help and work for my brother. The outcome was mediocre special education, an occupational therapy program that offered the opportunity to put pegs in holes, and a job as a maintenance worker at the local Saks Fifth Avenue department store, from which he eventually was fired. Throughout each of these ordeals, one constant remained in the face of Henry's humiliation and defeat: my mother's unrelenting care of and devotion to her son. But she, too, became defeated and ultimately retreated to the safer boundaries of house and family, turning to the blessed Madonna as her archetype of maternal compassion and sacrifice. She intuitively understood that she would never find an answer to her problem through a set of rational tools. My brother's condition became her cross to bear and secured in her a distinctly southern Italian response, fatalistic and religious to the point of martyrdom.

· · ·

*Y*OU MUST have a really strong mother," a young assistant editor at the *Voice* remarked to me one day as we stood by the restroom sink, the central place for girl talk at the paper.

The observation, announced out of the blue by someone who didn't know me but seemed extremely intuitive about mothers, startled me. I fiddled with the faucet, unsure of how to respond. She was the shy and literary daughter of a well-known feminist who wrote novels and essays about trapped women like my mother. Finding my way through the labyrinthine world of New York City politics working with the macho gang, I regarded my ambition and determination as a reaction to, not the fruit of, my mother's steady presence. The constant attention that my brother required, along with raising two other children, cooking, cleaning, and reentering the workforce as a typist to help pay for Bob's and my college tuition, ensured that my mother personified the opposite of a "free woman."

"I don't know . . . ," I mumbled and reached for the soap, momentarily washing my hands of the matter.

At the time, I couldn't tell her, or myself, the obvious answer to the question—yes, I do have a strong mother—because in my new world, strength through sacrifice was not a virtue applauded but a response considered weak and stereotypically female.

"You must really like to serve people," I once said to my mother with the cruel indifference to her feelings of which only a daughter may be capable.

"Not really," she answered with a nervous laugh.

Sacrificio, sacrifice, spilled from the lips of Italian-American women of my mother's generation like sugar poured into espresso as they resigned themselves to sweeten life's bitterness, usually at the expense of their own desires. From the point of view of a daughter whose mother stepped back, allowing me to step forward, I had no use for this servile female role. Inherent in any act of sacrifice is both beauty and destruction—the surrender of self to aid another—but I could see only loss in the equation, and questioned how anyone could spend a lifetime caught in this interlaced pas de deux. It wasn't until I became a mother that I better recognized how sacrifice, and its essential component compassion, are integral parts of life because no one is ever fully independent unless living in a fictive neverland of the never young, never sick, never old.

· · ·

*M*Y MODEL of maternal care was greatly skewed because a finite period of dependency stretched into a lifetime:

My brother's emotional behavior and learning abilities have stayed at the level of a young boy, so the burdens of dependency were never relieved. Those who have experienced the limitless demands of the disabled child are more sensitive to the giant holes in the American social service system, continually seeing how the world's richest industrialized country provides the least support to the young and needy.

Philosophy professor Eva Feder Kittay, who is the mother of a profoundly mentally retarded daughter, set forth a political theory in her book *Love's Labor: Essays on Women, Equality, and Dependency* to reconcile the conflict of dependency and equality in the lives of women. Kittay argues that equality-based policies have mostly failed women in the public and private sphere. Only a small number of women represent us politically, and whether working or at home full-time, women perform more than three-quarters of household chores and child-rearing responsibilities.

Kittay has put forth a concept of equality based on the simple and profound truth that everyone is "some mother's child," a phrase that recognizes the "fundamental connection between a mothering person and the fate of the individual she has mothered." Kittay rejects the notion of justice as individual or based on the premise that each person has a conception of the good and competes equally for resources (the starting point for John Rawls's famous theory). Instead she favors a "connection-based" equality, recognizing that at some point in life every person is dependent. Her formidable proposals point out the dilemmas of a feminism based on Enlightenment ideals and aim to shift the very language of Western philosophical thought from "I" to "we."

Kittay's theories reveal the intricate thinking of a philosopher and mother of a severely disabled daughter whose daily struggles have reinforced for her the reality that dependency and equality are mutually exclusive unless society offers resources for the dependent person and the one who provides the care. She challenges our cultural ethos that it's a woman's personal choice to have a child with the obvious rejoinder that if women didn't have children, society could not continue.

By replacing the credo of self-reliance with the goal of a common societal good, the responsibility of care is a principle to which any just and well-ordered society must aspire: "to each according to his or her need for care, from each according to his or her capacity for care, and such support from social institutions as to make available resources and opportunities to those providing care," writes Kittay.

Kittay proposes a theoretical rationale for paid family and medical leave, universal health care, more flexible work time, and better pay for dependency workers. Some of these benefits have long been adopted by countries that conservatives refer to as the coddled old Europe. Kittay reiterates the well-known fact that the (forever?) young United States is the most capable nation in the world of employing a public policy fairer to women and children but also the most recalcitrant.

Her boldest idea is payment for dependency work—a universally available, rationalized, and routinized payment such as worker's comp or unemployment—that would compensate mothers for their time caring for children or allow them to use the money for child care. "The encounter with dependency is rarely welcome to those fed an ideological diet of freedom, self-sufficiency, *and* equality," writes Kittay. "We have to use our multiple voices to expose the fiction and rebuild a world spacious enough to accommodate us all with our aspirations of a just and caring existence."

Women of my generation were raised on that diet, the lovely ideological truffle of having it all. So, many of us found ourselves a bit perplexed experiencing the emotional tug of balancing work with the reality of raising a child. The original feminist position paradoxically championed the rights of women while failing to satisfy the needs of mothers and children. In her book *The Equality Trap*, Mary Ann Mason, now dean of the graduate school at Berkeley, told of how the National Organization for Women and the National Women's Political Caucus filed a friend-of-the-court brief in the early Eighties *in favor* of the California Federal Savings and Loan after the bank fired a receptionist for taking a four-month *unpaid* maternity leave.

Fair is fair, the feminists argued; pregnant women should be treated the same as disabled men who under California law would not have been able to keep their jobs after a four-month leave. Similarly, courts created no-fault divorce in the name of equality, which left many middle-class women with children near poverty after the dust of the legal papers settled. Just as a divorced woman cannot adequately support her family if she earns a fraction of her former husband's salary, the situation of a new mother cannot be compared to one of a disabled man. The California receptionist was not requesting an unpaid leave to take care of herself but of a newborn.

Feminist thought too would evolve to question such concepts of liberal neutrality, and twenty years later the California branch of the National Organization for Women joined a large coalition of labor, community, and senior groups to support a paid family leave act, legislation that makes California one of three states in America to provide this benefit.

Yet the legacy of affirming equality without reconciling the reality of dependency has contributed to our country's shameful lack of family policies. Feminism also bought into the rhetoric of capitalism and rugged individualism, ensuring that American women as well as men can now work longer away from family than much of the rest of the world.

I used to think linearly, longing for the conclusive end of the sentence, a leap of faith that the future, not the past, offers the vital solution. But today my thought process feels circular, perhaps a crude version of Hegel's rhythm of history, that every idea posited needs also to be opposed. The feminist movement's historical and pivotal achievement was to create an antithesis to women's traditional subservience: autonomy against caregiving. But we still haven't found a sustainable synthesis of the two.

• • •

*M*Y FRIEND greets the mentally retarded man responsible for cleaning her neighborhood playground. He interprets her friendly hello as an entree into a longer conversation and stays by our side, unaware that the awkward pauses reflect a desire to talk among ourselves. It's the weekend of our twenty-fifth high school reunion, and my friend, recovering from a recent operation, has generously hosted a brunch for a few of us who now live in New York and Boston. We've left our crumbs on her dining room table and she rightly wants time to relax and talk while our children climb and slide. My friend tells the man politely but firmly that she's going to talk to us for a while. He quietly walks away.

Watching his head hang low, his eyes searching the ground with a well-honed loneliness, I know that I will eventually restart the conversation with him. I imagine injuries large and small inflicted by any person who has shunned this man or grown bored and irritated by his failure to recognize social cues. My childhood plays out before me: the memory of coming home from a supermarket with Henry one day, who lags behind me and walks fast to catch up. A man notices my brother's edges—crew cut, rail thin body, and fervent stare—and assumes that this figure threatens me.

"Is he bothering you? Do you want me to walk with you?" the man asks, cutting off my brother as he approaches me.

"No, no," I respond, humiliated that my trailing brother is confused for a dangerous man.

"What did he want, pigeon?" Henry asks a minute later.

"Nothing," I reply curtly, angry at everything: my brother, the man, suburban normalcy, and its stark absence in my life. So it is my nature to live in a city and carry on conversations with people who seem to be wounded sideline players in a life taking place around them.

A short time later, the mentally retarded man walks out of the playground's small equipment shed holding a navy rubber ball between his hands. Walking up to him, I ask him about the ball, the weather, any small talk that comes to mind. He has the worst set of yellowed false teeth I've ever seen. His upper plate lacks an adhesive, which causes his teeth to click and clatter each time his mouth opens, exposing the pink gums of a baby. The slipping teeth divert my attention from the conversation, for now I can focus only on these choppers as they dice words like a busy food processor and crumble sentences to meaningless letters. The man's hair is greasy, his uniform is dirty, and he looks in desperate need of a scrubbing.

Yet he is some mother's son. Is she still alive? She must no longer be capable of caring for him or he wouldn't look this way. Who is his family and how worn have they become supporting a life that needs constant supervision and care?

Because Henry is my mother's son, she takes him to the dentist for periodontal work to save teeth weakened by gum disease. Watching the man in the park, I think about my past frustrations with my mother's decisions, how she has seemed more concerned about addressing my brother's dental problems than the state of his mental health. But one is more easily fixed than the other, and as his mother she must care for him, washing his hair and combing out the tangles, placing his freshly laundered clothes on the bed for each new day.

Being a mother who in her eighties still does not want to disappoint, she agrees against her own best judgment to fulfill Henry's wishes. She lugs a large ladder up the stairs to wash all the windows in the house because Henry finds satisfaction in dust destroyed and a job well done. She will also climb the ladder for him because my brother lacks the coordination to steady himself and is prone to seizures. A few days later, a dark purple bruise covers her entire upper arm; the chorus of blood vessels that she ruptured by carrying the ladder frightens the eye, and we tilt our heads slightly upward when talking to her, not wishing to directly confront her vulnerability. In mothering Henry, she has always sided with her primal instincts, plumbing the depths of sacrifice's deep, dark core to the detriment of her own health.

* * *

*I*N THE HEART OF southern Italy, an impoverished eighteenth-century Neapolitan philosopher named Giambattista Vico sought to counter the values of Enlightenment rationalism, which he found coldly worshipful to the creed that truth was objective and was revealed purely through the laws of science. To Vico, the realists of his day who believed that math and science alone unfurled life's essence failed to understand the textured layers of human experience and the symbolic ways in which people have viewed the world and expressed themselves.

The Enlightenment thinker Voltaire championed progress through universal reason with his belief in an unaltering human nature and timeless truths that throughout history had been destroyed or corrupted by ignorant, brute people. Vico, on the other hand, possessed a broader psychological imagination, more finely attuned to the labyrinthine wants and desires of man, which led him to interpret history as the complicated movement of past and present, the curl and fold of a wave in an undulating, eternal ocean. Man is doomed to misunderstanding, argued Vico, if, instead of attempting to decipher the language and myths of the past as the expression of a particular time and people, he uses contemporary social and moral values to judge those who lived before. Vico didn't consider earlier societies merely unenlightened versions of our own more civilized world but rather self-contained civilizations, each possessing, like the Greece of Homer's poetry, its own powerful, frightening, and singular creations.

To Vico, there is no timeless natural law, a keystone to Enlightenment belief. Instead, each culture has its own unique form of expression. "Myths are not, as enlightened thinkers believe, false statements about reality corrected by later rational criticism, nor is poetry mere embellishment of what could equally well be stated in ordinary prose," wrote political philosopher Isaiah Berlin in an essay on Vico. Rather knowledge can begin to be obtained only by understanding nuances, how people used language, symbols, myths, and poetry to respond to the desires, fears, brutality, and hopes of their day.

As inheritors of an Enlightenment vision of history, we optimistically assume that a vigorous and certain march toward progress continues, as long as barriers like ignorance and superstition are removed from its path. America's myth of the melting pot extols this belief—that shortly after the early immigrants came here, they adopted the values and mores of the younger, stronger, ultimately more capable culture, and success was based upon their ability to assimilate. The notion that people would no longer live by, teach, or pass along the values upon which they were raised was, of course, absurd, but it was nonetheless a fiction absorbed by the culture until only fairly recently challenged by the emerging voices of African-Americans, Latinos, and Asians.

Yet any hyphenated American will feel, if attuned to the notes voiced by her relatives and ancestors, the pull and tug of these competing values. For better or for worse, Italian-Americans think about personal sacrifice differently than many Americans, viewing it as they do through the prism of their particular culture and past. Life and sacrifice were synonymous for impoverished southern Italian peasants, a daily fight for food and survival. As the communion host dissolved on the tongue, Catholicism reinforced that pain and suffering were inextricably bound to the hope of transcendence. Nothing was considered stronger or more important than blood ties, and honor was found in family responsibilities, not individual achievement.

My parents, in good southern Italian tradition, placed no limits on the sacrifices they made, or what they would expect of Bob and me. As we grew older, and the contrast in our abilities sharpened, my brother and I were denied the pleasures that eluded Henry. Henry, who loved cars and could name every model that GM produced, was not capable of driving, which meant that my brother and I couldn't drive in suburbia. Henry could not do well in school, so it was better not to acknowledge our academic achievements. "You know we're proud of you," was the most my parents offered. Only sending us off to college didn't fit into this pattern of self-sacrifice.

Henry could not get married and have children; therefore, my brother and I were denied the pleasure and the ability to discuss the future. I would announce a boyfriend with the same trepidation that my gay friends faced when they came out of the closet to their parents. Accepting my marriage was a complicated, heartbreaking struggle, as my parents clung to the past, refusing to admit that the only certainty in life is knowing that it will change. This reality hit my mother with the cruel force of a sudden gust of wind.

My mother's sacrifice places a tremendous burden on her, which will eventually be handed to my brother and me, a reality that wakes me from a peaceful night's sleep. My parents' decisions were limited and flawed, but they did the best they could within the boundaries imposed by their culture, religion, income, and what society had to offer. The beauty and pain of parenting a child is tenderly laying the bricks of self-confidence, ability, and independence upon which he'll eventually walk, creating the steady foundation to leave the family who raised him. But what if the child is damaged? Someone must make the sacrifice; the mother usually approaches the altar first, and stays for the duration.

· · ·

*Y*ou must have a really strong mother," the feminist's shy daughter remarked to me nearly twenty years ago. Back then, I was incapable of understanding a fundamental truth of human relationships—that the sacrifice of one can be a gift to another. This is a gift that American culture, fixated on personal achievement and unbridled prosperity, takes more and more for granted.

My friend, the poet and writer Wallis Wilde-Menozzi, moved to Parma, Italy, two decades ago with her Italian husband and their daughter. Her memoir, *Mother Tongue*, describes the cultural chasm she experienced between the values of her American birthplace and her newly adopted land. In a moving chapter on the death of her mother-in-law from cancer, she wrote about the decision of her husband, the chairman of the biology department at the University of Parma, to wipe clean his schedule once he learned of his mother's illness.

"He canceled all conferences. He decided he would give her medicine or baths or whatever was needed, day or night.

He started cooking to tempt her to take a mouthful or two. His colleagues concurred. They left him alone or caught him during his kamikaze visits to his office. What is the distance between cultures? What is it like—that freedom that starts so early in the States—where a mother and father want you to become . . . to go. Why would it seem unnatural to give over an unmeasured amount of time to someone who is dying?"

Wilde-Menozzi has observed Italian behavior in a prosperous and resourceful part of the land, unlike the poorer south where sacrifice dwells in the absence of other options. She mused in an essay about a Parma grandmother, a psychiatrist and mother of six, who proudly reported on her three-year-old granddaughter's precocious insights: "Her little mind hums like a top. You know what she said? 'My mother was in your stomach. And I was in her stomach. And so I was a little bit in your stomach.' "

"That beautiful continuity—that strong rooted space for the most basic and traditional links—is one reason Italy seduces in powerful and authentic ways," writes Wilde-Menozzi. "Human relations have as much space as work, and professionalism has different dimensions in terms of being a role. Family is not a sacrifice but an inevitable part of life, with its discomforts and adjustments, but also with its rewards of continuity, and the pleasure of knowing people through time, and having the right and privilege of taking care of them."

* * *

$\mathcal{O}$VER THE DECADE after I had gotten married and given birth to our son, I began to feel very Italian—that is, within me a deeply protective mamma was emerging who seemed ready to dictate the course of my new life. I wondered whether sacrifice would become for me, as it had for my own mother, my maternal model. I couldn't follow the same path; I would have to try to find a comfortable place for myself amid the hum of two dominant, divergent traditions: a fatalistic Mediterranean culture in which familial dependence is prized and a ruggedly individualistic American culture that neglects its needy dependents, young and old.

In the early years of caring for my son, I was eager to read—when I could find time to relax and keep my eyes open—books about the work-family conflict. Yet I became frustrated with two schools of thought that I continually came across, both of which seemed equally simplistic: one that urged women to stay home and enjoy the beauties of maternity, and one that sought to justify a woman's full-time work as beneficial to a child's development.

To me, the first was yet another replay of an age-old argument that has denied women the opportunity to use their gifts in a wider world than the family home. The second, that little is lost in family life when two parents work lengthy days, frustrated me even more because this belief was articulated by people like myself; yet once I had a child, it was a belief that I could no longer share. In caring for my son, my heart leads and has intuited a false note in this assertion. Surely, I thought feminists were conflating two values, making either a narcissistic assumption that our children's needs are identical with our own desires, or a naive one, untested by any difficult life experience, that personal ambition and the nurturing of others can march smoothly hand in hand.

"Everything is what it is, liberty is liberty, not equality or fairness or justice or culture, or human happiness or a quiet conscience," wrote Isaiah Berlin, who pondered throughout his life the need to make choices and to sacrifice some values to others.

2

Mothers

Intermezzo:
Light and Shade

*D*AVID CHASE, the Italian-American creator of *The Sopranos*, posed questions that every dutiful ethnic son and daughter at some point ponders. He answered them darkly:

Q: What happens if you put your mother in a nursing home? A: She'll take out a contract on your life. Q: Do you care for your senile and delusional uncle when your self-involved siblings refuse to help? A: Only if you want him to pull out a gun and put you in a coma.

One wonders what Chase's answer might be to the question, What happens if you leave your child with a babysitter and go to work? But he didn't ask it; he's a guy. And luckily for Tony Soprano, his therapist, Dr. Melfi, had no little one to care for. There were no illnesses or school celebrations that might have forced her to cancel a session with her infamous client.

* * *

*T*HE TROUBLE didn't start until we had our babies," my friend Joanna remarked to me one Sunday afternoon as we shared a long, leisurely lunch in my apartment. Joanna, a writer and teacher, is also Italian-American and fifteen years older than I am. After growing up in Waterbury, Connecticut, in a traditional, extended southern Italian family, Joanna came to New York in the Sixties to attend graduate school and soon became involved in the early days of the feminist movement. Joanna reminisced about the initial thrill of her consciousness-raising group as women began to lay the path for gender equality in living rooms across the country. "Here we were fighting for civil rights, protesting the war, but we were still making the coffee."

Joanna was in her mid-thirties when she gave birth to her son James. To her surprise, she found herself being pulled back to her southern Italian heritage and traditions. She'd always been keenly aware that she grew up in a "sealed Italian existence"—the isolated mountainous region of Basilicata, the home of her grandparents, transported here. But after her son was born, Joanna began to think of herself first and foremost as an Italian woman raising a child. Joanna put aside several days a week to write in the library at New York University, but she ended up taking the first year off. Having wanted to be a mother since she was a little girl, she found herself unable to focus on anything else. "He was the total center and I couldn't hold two centers at the same time," Joanna explained.

Southern Italian cultural and religious icons also began to emerge from the recesses of her memory and color her vision. The celebration of holidays took on a greater significance. Finding herself drawn to the figure of the Virgin Mary, she started to read canonical and noncanonical texts about the saint: "I thought to myself, mother-to-mother, she understands me." Joanna and her husband may have chosen to live in Greenwich Village in the Eighties, but the Madonna she called upon was not the one singing "Like a Virgin."

I find it easy to talk with Joanna. We can converse for hours at a time because both of us were raised with similar southern Italian values. We still struggle with some of the customs and at various times in our lives have either rebelled against or embraced them. When we swapped stories about the first year after our sons were born—I wrote part-time and felt less guilty leaving the house than she did—Joanna suggested that feminism's accomplishments in the fifteen years between us had made a large difference in how we perceived ourselves and place in the world. "Feminism came too late in my ethnic life," Joanna said, "the codes were already so embedded in me."

Hearing her words, I felt fortunate to have benefited from the sweeping inroads feminists had made, as well as having been able to create my own work schedule in those early years. Joanna and I both think about care from an Italian-American perspective. The expectations placed upon us—not only for our children but parents and siblings too—have often been so impossibly high to meet that, as Joanna remarked, "the bottom line is that you always fail."

Yet no matter how much my friend has tried to leave behind her birthplace, she believes that its vitality and uniqueness have never found an equal in her Manhattan life. And James's birth solidified Joanna's intuitive belief that, despite her early rebellion, the ancient culture of her grandparents with its "Homeric ideas of pride and honor, shame and hospitality, of singing and storytelling" could never be left fully behind.

* * *

*A*UTONOMY IS only the mirror image of dependence on others," Japanese novelist Haruki Murakami wisely wrote. "If you were left as a baby on a deserted island, you would have no notion of what 'autonomy' means. Autonomy and dependency are like light and shade, caught in the pull of each other's gravity, until, after considerable trial and error, each individual can find his or her own place in the world."

Today with James earning a Ph.D. in neuroscience, he shares with his mother a scientist's perspective on how embedded these behavioral and emotional codes indeed may be. Neuroscientists are discovering how the brain, with billions of neurons from our nervous system firing it signals, in turn constructs models of the world to shape and guide our behavior. As Joanna excitedly discussed some of James's work with me, I was reminded of the role of biology and evolutionary behavior in this pull and tug of autonomy and dependency, the light and shade by which we live. And although the sun was already setting from our long afternoon together, I realized that there was one more story that I, too, needed to share.

Our Bellies, Ourselves

WHEN I WAS four months pregnant, I began a weekly prenatal yoga class held in a town house a short walk from where we lived. The criterion for eligibility, besides, of course, our flowering selves, was that the women needed to have completed their first trimester, a quarter moon's sliver poking through the dark breadth of spandex, to enroll. The town house had a small shop on the first floor that sold yoga and spirituality books with pictures of white-robed gurus seated beneath flaming orange sunsets. Books that made me nervous, as if their mere jackets could transform a passerby into a head-shaven cult member who stuffs quarters in her pockets for afterlife preparation. Books that reminded me of a conversation with my mother some years before.

"Do you still do that yoga?"

"I haven't for a while."

"I told your father that's what took you away from Catholicism."

I didn't know that I had left Catholicism, but felt less easy each time I passed the let-*us*-help-yourself literature while swishing my soggy snow boots to the chant of "Nama Shivaya" on cassette.

I had first started taking yoga classes when I was in my late twenties and lived in a tiny studio apartment in Manhattan. At the time, I was searching for some calm in the city and balance in the suburbs when I visited my family. I was trying to find a metered gauge, like the valve on a gas pump, that could pour forth emotional truths; too little sacrifice and we stall from selfish inertia; too much and the overflow catches fire.

I needed to relax. Be happy. Breathe.

And soon I longed for that deep stretch and inhalation to counter life's increasingly cramped and breathless moments. My mother, on the other hand, believed that practicing yoga meant pulling the rug of Old World tradition from beneath my feet and replacing it with some squishy mat of half-baked, incense-laden new age thought. Better not to tell her that the exercise preached a body-breath-mind trinity or she would have felt certain that I had traded in our established Western dogma for an inferior Indian import.

Yoga was but one small step of rebellion in my leap toward independence from the old ways. Longing to be a thoroughly modern Maria, I assumed that, except in name, I had no connection to my grandmothers Maria or the life that once took root in the winemaking basement and aromatic kitchen of

.gfield Avenue. I scoffed at the homemade remedies
𝗎 along to my mom; they could have been brewed by an
old Italian *strega*, those southern witch goddesses who con-
cocted cures for doctorless villages. I would abandon those
homemade cures along with a list of old wives' tales handed
down with the foolproof certainty of generations.

No longer would I believe that sitting on a damp stoop or
leaving the house with wet hair brought on a cold, or that the
cure for most ills could be found not in a doctor's office but in
a bottle of Witch Hazel. I climbed stone steps streaked white
from winter's chill, plunked myself down with liberated glee,
and audaciously proclaimed myself rebel of the rear.

But on my way to the floor mat, I never stumbled upon
a contradiction that perhaps should have been more obvious. New age wisdom, of which yoga has become a main-
stay, sprang from a similar Old World source—a back-to-basic
belief in your body that scorned and feared modernity, like science and medicine. Breathe, focus, stretch—the philosophy
of yoga revealed—and the truths of the universe, as well as my
body's place within it, would slowly unfold.

This frame of mind was fine for my twenty-something self
lunging the evening away, but when I became pregnant at
thirty-seven it took a dangerous turn. By pursuing a natural
approach to pregnancy, fueled by a powerful feminist belief
in the autonomy of the female body, I unwittingly put myself
on a highly dangerous course. I was more intimately linked to
those southern Italian women than I had ever dreamed.

The chilly white-streaked plank upon which one sits in
defiance of the past can be as deceiving as what is in your

neighbor's eye but not your own. Or, put another way, maybe I needed to get off my *asana* and smell the coffee. But even my favorite aroma made me ill in my second trimester.

. . .

$\mathcal{P}$URCHASING A prenatal yoga ticket on a chilly winter morning, I received a rectangular piece of laminated blue cardboard to enter a room called Heaven. The eight dollar fee seemed a small price for pre-maternal bliss. I skipped the stairway to Heaven and waited for the slow, narrow elevator (aren't the gates always narrow?) to bring me to a bright and inviting space.

How did I get here? I wondered. Not to Heaven, but back to yoga after so many years, this time as a pregnant woman. I used to stare at the dark ceiling on sleepless nights and plan speeches to my husband about my difficult childhood, the exhausting struggle for a life of my own, and my subsequent reluctance to have a child. But in my mid-thirties something began to happen—everyone around me was having babies. When someone once remarked that I would like a certain resort because the "childless beautiful people" stayed there, I bristled. Was that how I was seen by others: a sybarite, not a potential self-sacrificing mom? Make a mother out of a self-indulgent woman, the philosopher William James once commented, and see how she is transformed: "Possessed by maternal excitement, she now confronts wakefulness, weariness, and toil without an instant of hesitation or word of complaint."

I didn't think being childless was self-indulgent but rather a fact shaped by forces outside of one's control or a realistic

understanding of one's own limitations. I feared my limitations, and was saddled with a limited imagination.

Yet other feelings emerged too: I enjoyed watching our
friends' babies grow into toddlers. A budding curiosity replaced
the boredom I once felt around new mothers, and I realized
that awkwardness and fear had framed much of my ambivalence. The possibility gradually unfolded that raising a child
could differ from the experience of raising my eldest brother,
so I began to imagine holding my own baby (I also imagined dropping him on his soft spot, but tried not to go there).
Sheepishly, uncertainly, I asked to hold other people's babies.
And if I could cuddle without causing a catastrophic spill,
could I do anything else too? It's perhaps impossible to pin-
point the time when reasoning switches, and I began thinking
about adding a new life into ours instead of imagining how the
freedoms we had enjoyed would be taken away.

· · ·

I TRIED to soak up Heaven's calm, stretching coil-tight
tendons, ballooning my baby belly with deep breaths, and hoping peace could flow like oxygen and nourish my new body.
Imprinted on my wrinkled black T-shirt, chosen from a forgotten pile on a high closet shelf, were soothing celestial blue
Japanese characters that matched the color of my ticket and
spelled out the words "Ten Thousand Waves."

My dog-eared pregnancy books told me that I couldn't enter
a hot tub for nine months. But my T-shirt allowed me to drift
back to Ten Thousands Waves, a Sante Fe spa, and remember
how the water steamed my body as I rested my head against

the rim of a wooden tub, offering my face to the chill of a starry night. Looking up from my mat, I saw another woman arrive wearing the same T-shirt, and the sight of our mirrored chests doused my new serenity with the clarity of a bucket of cold water: What kind of person buys spa souvenirs?

The teacher's body was strong and lean, and her generically accented yoga voice, deep and butter smooth, instructed us in a relaxed, rhythmic cadence. As she led about a dozen pregnant women, knees bent, arms stretched in Warrior One pose, the teacher told her own birthing story, how a midwife guided her delivery at home. She said that deep breathing and massage made a natural birth without anesthetic not only a feasible experience but a transforming one.

The details of her story ran through my mind like those tiny books of sequential photos found in tourist shops; with a rapid flip of the thumb, a mini-movie appears. I imagined a midwife in a dimly lit room, her sturdy arms kneading, rocking, massaging the body of the mother, who moaned, breathed, pushed and—crescendo! Warrior Two!—tiny limbs appeared and out popped a baby. End of book. Sounded almost easy, inviting. I decided to come back for this weekly class of exercise and encouragement.

In an effort to learn a little about our group, as new faces entered and old ones delivered, the yoga teacher asked a few questions about our pregnancies. Did we know the gender? When were our due dates? Where would we deliver?

"Mount Sinai," said one woman.

"Columbia Presbyterian," announced another.

"The Elizabeth Seton Childbirthing Center," said several women.

"Great!" replied the teacher.

Elizabeth Seton, which has since closed because of the skyrocketing costs of medical malpractice insurance premiums, was a birthing center affiliated with a hospital that used midwives and offered minimal anesthesia.

"Anyone having a home birth?" the teacher asked.

Not this week's group; perhaps the next. I imagined the perfect prenatal yoga student to answer, "Home birth in water."

"I'm having an obstetrician deliver my baby," one woman said a bit meekly and defensively in a class that had weighed heavily with the midwifery model.

"I'm fifty and this is my first baby," she added, feeling the need to explain why she chose a doctor. The woman looked almost a decade younger than her age, and the class let out a muted gasp, intrigued that we were sharing pillows and mats with someone who was a hairbreadth from menopause yet preparing to have a baby.

We clapped and assured her that her decision was correct.

I was somewhere in the middle of this group, not mentally limber enough to bend with the magnetic flow of energy that could completely eliminate the need for a doctor. I was labeled "low risk" by my obstetrician's practice but was also an AMA, the discreet acronym for advanced maternal age. Although I wanted my doctor, whom I had known for years and trusted, to be with me in the delivery room, I was informed that I would have to use a midwife because the doctors in this practice were assigned only to "high risk" women.

My doctor assured me that I was better off with a midwife, who had the time and skill to work with me in a birthing room and wouldn't use forceps, as a hurried physician might. New

York, with its research hospitals and aggressive medical culture, was behind the rest of the country in the acceptance and understanding of midwives, my doctor told me. Pregnancy should not be treated as an illness. As a soon-to-be mother, not a patient, I would retain my dignity, autonomy, and massage oil.

Yet despite all this talk about the nurturing philosophy of midwifery, even my doctor admitted that managed care played a part in her group's decision: It was cheaper to hire midwives than additional doctors in a practice that received a fixed amount of money per delivery from health maintenance organizations.

I was also skeptical because I knew the fragility of those first moments of life, having lived the reality of the botched delivery of my brother. Science comforted me. Yet I also liked yoga and trusted nurturing feminist doctors like mine, who began her career wearing Birkenstocks in a Chinatown hospital and now had an all-women practice housed in a large partitioned loft, brightly painted in the waiting area but kept standard white for the examining rooms.

I told the yoga class that I would deliver with a midwife at a local hospital.

. . .

WHILE MY MOTHER treated more aches, bites, and pains with Witch Hazel than I thought possible for one bottle of astringent, made us "sweat out" fevers until the sheets and blankets were drenched, prepared gargles of salt and water, and considered the remedy for an earache an oven-heated cloth, even she wouldn't have delivered her children the Old World way, using a midwife instead of a doctor. But how a woman delivers her baby is essentially a public act, dictated by the prevailing beliefs of the culture. My mother followed the practices of her generation, receiving pain medication during labor only when the doctor offered, and later wondering how she had managed her earlier births without the epidural pain block.

She abandoned the messy breast for the tidy bottle because her generation associated breast feeding with a peasant, not middle-class mentality. Because I was bottle fed, I'm sure that my fervent insistence to breast-feed came from today's knowledge that a mother's milk is best for the baby, although I had to supplement my meager milk supply once a day by hanging a plastic bottle around my neck that dripped formula into tiny tubes taped to both my nipples.

Each generation adapts and adopts, embracing and rejecting cultural norms depending on the individual and collective consciousness of its time. Drug-free deliveries, welcomed by feminists in the latter half of the twentieth century, were scorned by feminists at the beginning of that century because they were considered the brutish response of male doctors who wanted to see women suffer.

The notion of pregnancy as an all-natural phenomenon that rarely justifies medical intervention is a deeply rooted cultural belief, as Dr. Donald Caton pointed out in his informative book about the history of pain management in childbirth, *What a Blessing She Had Chloroform*. In the nineteenth century, physicians were wary of administering anesthesia for a variety of medical and social reasons. The risks of chloroform and other drugs were still unknown, and although a century had passed since the Puritan dominance of Cotton Mather, seeds of such moralism endured. Mather, a pillar of early American religious sensibility, had admonished laboring women to recall Eve and remember that "The Sin of my Mother which is also my Sin, has brought all this upon me!"

Yet by the nineteenth century some women, like Fanny Appleton Longfellow, sought relief. Fanny, wife of the poet Henry Wadsworth Longfellow, was the first woman to receive anesthesia during childbirth in the United States; she requested ether during the birth of her third child, a daughter, in 1847. She wrote to her sister-in-law shortly after the birth: "I am very sorry you all thought me so rash and naughty in trying the ether. Henry's faith gave me courage, and I had heard such a thing had succeeded abroad, where the surgeons extend this great blessing more boldly and universally than our timid doctors." Fanny, in fact, had to convince a dentist to give her ether because she couldn't find an American physician willing to administer anesthesia during childbirth.

It would take until the next century before obstetricians began to dissent from the prevailing view that medication was unnecessary and harmful. A group of pro-anesthesia obstetricians found an ally in feminist Elizabeth Cady Stanton, who challenged the widespread belief that rich women's delicate bodies were more susceptible to pain than those of peasant women, and who lambasted a system that denied poor women access to pain relief medication during labor. In Stanton's time, the use of anesthesia during pregnancy was an important feminist issue; decades later, Virginia Woolf also advocated chloroform during labor in her book *Three Guineas*, considering the drug a progressive, commonsense measure to help all women.

Twilight Sleep—the knock-'em-out-until-the-baby-is-born drug that mixed morphine and scopolamine—was first championed as a panacea to the curse of childbearing by a small group of women who traveled to Germany to obtain the drug combination, which was not offered in America.

But sides shifted again later in the twentieth century as heavy doses of drugs like Twilight Sleep became dangerous for both the mother and the newborn. Writers Doris Lessing and Sylvia Plath described appalling stories of these narcotics, which robbed mothers of the childbirth experience and left them depressed and debilitated. "The white dome of chloroform," in Lessing's words, was lowered over the face of a wailing woman, turning the memories of her baby's birth into a bad dream. Feminists, horrified by controlling doctors who forced women into metal stirrups, and hospital environments that isolated drugged mothers from their babies, turned to the methods of natural childbirth. By the 1970s the home birth movement, which urged women to declare sovereignty over their bodies, began to bloom.

Emily Martin used a Marxist analogy of alienation in *The Women in the Body*, describing insensitive doctors as workplace managers and women as oppressed laborers estranged from their own bodily functions. The ultimate strike? Have a home birth.

In her 1982 book *In Labor*, Barbara Katz Rothman argued that women had been coerced into accepting situations that benefited doctors more than mothers. Medical management searches for pathology, Rothman argued, whereas midwifery approaches pregnancy as normal and healthy. "I learned that hospitals have never been demonstrated to be the safest place for a woman to give birth," she wrote. "I learned that hospitals pose unique dangers for birthing women and their babies, including the overuse of medication, higher risk of infection, and numerous obstetrical interferences in the physiological process of birth."

Rothman concluded her sweeping embrace of midwifery by suggesting that even if a small number of babies died from being born at home, it was acceptable for the greater goal of the home birth movement: "The medical profession has of late made it standard practice to try and save every baby born, and we have seen in recent years the proliferation of neonatal intensive-care units. . . . Possibly because midwives are not trained with the idea that their work is a struggle against death, it is possible for them to take a more balanced view of the death of a baby."

A more balanced view? I was one of many women who didn't have the luxury of testing Rothman's perspective; I and my son needed all that science had to offer.

It seems a peculiarly American phenomenon that at a time when the National Organization for Women was arguing against mothers taking unpaid maternity leave because equality in the workplace was more important than nurturing at home, another strain of feminist thinking found its voice in midwifery, natural childbirth, and the home birth movement. Advocating for natural childbirth was an embrace of Old World customs with a decidedly New World twist—an exaltation of the self at the pinnacle of a woman's life.

These feminists distrusted the Enlightenment's unswerving faith in science while championing the movement's more emotive side—the Rousseauian not the Voltairian strain—which glorified, as Terry Eagleton put it, "cults of the self, the inner light, inward experience, authenticity, and autobiography." (Rousseau was an early proponent of breast feeding—nature's way, as he saw it. He wove silk ribbons and gave them to girls about to marry who promised to breast-feed their babies rather than hand them over to a wet nurse. He had, however, a more unnatural relationship with his own children, abandoning all five to a foundling hospital at their birth.)

Clearly the seduction of returning to an earlier time, the rejection of modernity's oppressive sterility, couldn't have found a more suitable place than in the home birth movement. Women, not the patriarchal arm of medicine, should determine how they would undertake this most primal act. Proponents of natural childbirth preferred to eliminate medicine and the IV in the birthing room in favor of homey cures such as massage oil, cornstarch, honey, lemon slices, a tennis ball, and a rolling pin, to name just a few items included on my childbirthing class's xeroxed sheet of "What to bring to the hospital." (I never did figure out at what stages the tennis ball and the rolling pin were used; I couldn't help imagining they might be taken out for an impromptu ball game.)

Because the midwifery model granted women more individual control over the birthing process, it became a "feminist" project. But as Susan Maushart pointed out in *The Mask of Motherhood*, despite all the emphasis placed today on childbirth teaching, women's anxieties are not diminishing. "They have merely been refocused," writes Maushart. "So that where our mothers and grandmothers worried about physical survival, we obsess about emotional style."

Today, as doctors use smaller doses of anesthesia that don't seem to affect the baby, women have achieved the right to choose how they wish to deliver, and the majority opt for drugs. Still, at the end of nine months, one question records a woman's battle in the story of her life, the method by which she approaches the rocky terrain of her own private Anzio. The decision that divides—which camp will you choose?—and ultimately conquers: the decision whose vast complexities get reduced and contained in the raised-eyebrow cadence of the unavoidable, inescapable welcome to the maternity club question. Did you get the epidural?

*   *   *

 As the chill of early spring began to subside and a crevice of April sunlight arrived, I hastened my preparations to become a mother. Tony and I enrolled in an evening childbirthing class with a teacher named Michelle. A small woman with thick loops of blond hair that framed her round face, Michelle had the energy of a preschool teacher and a bouncy, almost dizzying manner. She constantly interrupted herself, jumping up to grab assorted pens, repeatedly circling topics on her charts like a pilot approaching a crowded landing strip.

Michelle held up charts with bumps and hills marked with felt-tipped pens that were supposed to represent the cycles of labor. But I found them confusing and I ignored them, assuming I'd instinctively figure things out. She hinted that a delivery without anesthesia is better for the mother and the baby because drugs can cause complications. And if Michelle's points about drugs were missed during class, we'd be reminded of them when reading her handouts at home. One, entitled "Pain Medication without a Needle," advised laboring women to "sway, rock, dance to keep your pelvis mobile."

During those weeks, Tony and I endlessly discussed an epidural versus going it alone. I was very nervous. Should I put my glad rags on and rock around the contractions or take the cowardly approach and demand drugs? I was willing to question medicine for the hard-fought principles of feminism. Trying to face my fear, I absorbed the recurrent theme of classes and books and their abundantly clear message: Women who forgo anesthesia to deliver naturally are rewarded with an inimitable experience by achieving an almost mystical sovereignty over their bodies.

Yet in the middle of a walking tour of the hospital's birthing rooms, I heard the feral shrieking and wailing of a woman in labor. For some bizarre reason, the woman's screams blared through a set of speakers in the waiting area where we were listening to an instructor discuss pleasant tales of the postbirth lobster meal. My husband, who can be artful in his practice of denial, thought the shrieking was part of a television show. I, on the other hand, having tuned in to the piercing, animalistic cries, found it hard to return to the lobster channel.

In another class with Michelle, we sat on the floor in a circle and passed around small vials of eucalyptus oil, which everyone inhaled. It was a moment of transcendence that, two decades earlier, would have included the Grateful Dead. Michelle then massaged one woman's legs, instructing the small group of jittery husbands who until this moment had been a government manager, an abstract painter, and a struggling actor but would soon become coaches, deep breathers, and birthing partners.

Massage oil was high on Tony's hospital packing list, which he carefully organized on the computer, printed, and placed in a thick notebook that included projected timetables and baby furniture receipts. The notebook resembled the one he produced a year earlier for our kitchen renovation project, and we secretly hoped that our son would arrive as efficiently as the convection oven did.

Childbirthing class was our weekly highlight, but the other participants began to exit more quickly than anyone had anticipated. One couple left because the wife had an earlier-than-expected delivery. We lost another couple when the wife was ordered on bed rest because of a lack of fluid in the placenta. Despite the emphasis on nature, things weren't flowing too naturally.

At thirty-three weeks pregnant, I arrived at class one evening with terrible neck and shoulder pains. Michelle, who regularly offered homemade remedies for a variety of pregnancy ailments, found a man's gym sock, which she filled with sprigs of dried lavender and warmed for me in a microwave. The gym sock sachet exuded a curious, sweaty odor, like a crowded Parisian metro in July. But the horseshoe around my neck soothed the pain, and Michelle encouraged me to bring it home. Maybe all I needed was a hot gym sock stuffed with this Mediterranean herb plus a splash of cold Witch Hazel—a pregnancy cure that could have been torn from the recipe book of a *strega*.

· · ·

I DECIDED to call a midwife in my doctor's practice to tell her about the shoulder ache that, even with Michelle's warm gym sock, wouldn't abate, along with a bad headache I suffered a few nights before, and a pain in my upper abdomen.

"Take Tylenol," the midwife advised. But if my shoulder continued to hurt, she abruptly added, I should see an internist.

I had never met the internist whom I had chosen from a managed care plan, but based on recommendations and his affiliation with the highly regarded New York Hospital, I called his office to describe the pain.

"The doctor is booked, but we have walk-in hours," the receptionist told me.

I headed straight to New York Hospital and soon learned that "walk-in" hours meant a clinic staffed with residents. After an hour sitting next to very sick elderly people, one of whom coughed and wheezed so hard in a bathroom that a staff member threatened to break open the door, I met a young ob-gyn resident. She gently rubbed my shoulder and offered her medical opinion: Go to Bloomingdale's and buy a firmer pillow, and get a pregnancy massage. Relax and indulge in the beauty of my belly. Because of her inexperience, she forgot to take my blood pressure, but I followed doctor's orders and left the hospital on a slow walk to Bloomingdale's.

Two days later, we joined a few friends who toasted my thirty-fourth week with sparkling water. I was feeling sluggish walking to the restaurant, but then, in my eighth month, that was to be expected.

I awoke the next morning, lifted my head from my firm new pillow, and felt something plump and moist in my mouth. Running my finger along my gums, I extracted what I imagined was a stray chickpea from my eggplant and chickpea dinner of the night before. Or did I eat grapes before going to bed? But instead I dislodged a large clump of blood.

As more slimy clumps oozed from my mouth, I ran to the bathroom sink, imagining that I was bleeding internally. I dialed my doctor and begged the answering service to locate her. My husband, already at his office when I called him, grabbed a cell phone, hailed a taxi, and kept me on the line until he got home. With still no word from my doctor, Tony telephoned our managed care plan to tell them we were going to the emergency room. At the time, he was helping run a not-for-profit health maintenance organization, and he knew the drill of managed care.

"I'm sorry but my wife is too sick to talk to you," he told the plan's nurse, whose job is to reduce expensive hospital visits by reassuring people to wait for their own doctor. At the hospital, a nervous young emergency room attendant led me to the maternity ward, where a nurse took my blood pressure, which was high. About a half hour later, my doctor's partner walked into the room where I lay, reprimanding me for going to the hospital instead of her office and refusing to believe that no one had called me back. My exasperated midwife had already called the hospital and angrily asked the nurse, who stretched the phone cord over my belly to speak to her, "What is she doing there?"

Both the Partner and the midwife considered me an over-wrought pregnant woman who probably needed to have a dentist check my bleeding gums. My own medical chart marked my predisposition to nervousness: Two weeks earlier, during a routine checkup, another doctor was concerned about the pace of the fetal heartbeat and hooked me up to a monitor. As I lay there, thinking about how every man on my mother's side of the family suffered from heart trouble, I became so agitated that faint contractions began.

That morning, however, I knew that my condition was not about nerves. My body was screaming for help, and although I recoiled after being yelled at by a doctor, still I was glad to be in a hospital bed.

During the next two hours, my blood pressure soared to 188 over 110 (my gums were oozing blood because my pressure was so high), my kidneys and liver were shutting down, my forearms turned black and blue as my veins spasmed and rejected IV needle after needle, and my blood was failing to clot. I was diagnosed with the most severe form of the pregnancy disorder preeclampsia—the cause of which is still unknown and the only cure is to deliver the baby, no matter how early in gestation. The preeclampsia syndrome I had was aptly named HELLP, which stands for *h*emolysis (the destruction of red blood cells that eventually starves the body of oxygen), *e*levated *l*iver enzymes, and *l*ow *p*latelet count.

The Partner summed up the test results: "You have a life-threatening condition. We have to operate immediately."

I shrieked.

"Emote later," said the Partner. There was a lot of information to process, she told me, and I needed to listen to every word.

Emote later? For this I had chosen a feminist practice and its band of caring midwives? Years later, having requested my hospital chart, I saw the Partner's interpretation of her role during that dreadful moment: "Patient seems upset," she wrote. "Reassurance offered."

By then, I was perilously close to making the deadly transition from preeclampsia to full-blown eclampsia, the onset of seizures and coma. If my soaring blood pressure had been left untreated, it could have led to a stroke caused by a bursting artery in the brain. In a normal pregnancy, a woman's placental blood vessels widen, but my vessels had constricted or become blocked, preventing them from nourishing the fetus, weakening the blood supply to my organs, and sending my body into chaos.

"You don't know how lucky you are that you got yourself to the hospital this morning," whispered a nurse who had heard the midwife and Partner ridicule me.

A perinatologist suggested putting off an emergency C-section to stabilize my blood pressure and induce me into labor. When the induction failed, there was no choice but to have the C-section, despite the danger of operating on someone whose blood wasn't clotting. My own doctor came on duty later that evening and, with her characteristic diligence and sensitivity, seamlessly performed the surgery. I had enough blood platelets working to prevent the need for a transfusion, or my bleeding to death, which can also happen with severe preeclampsia. My baby and I fully recovered.

Luckily, thankfully, God help us gratefully, the quick and skilled hospital intervention allowed me and my newborn son to escape the tragic outcome of undiagnosed severe preeclampsia, which I would later research in medical texts. Phrases such as "snowball crashing down a hill" and "fallen over the cliff" are used to describe preeclampsia's often unpredictable and fast progression. By now, I have read too many newspaper features and Web site accounts that fly in the face of medical progress with numbing stories of premature babies too young to survive, stillbirths, and women who died in the

weeks after giving birth or remained in a coma for days, sometimes months.

Preeclampsia affects about one in twenty women. The far
more severe HELLP syndrome occurs in about 5 percent of
preeclampsia patients and is fatal in about nine deaths per
100,000 births. Yet what these numbers don't reveal, explains
Mike Rich, chief executive of the British organization Action
on Pre-Eclampsia, are "the near misses. A lot of women come
within a hair's breadth of dying."

The Partner was even more blunt when she ran into us
the first time I was allowed to visit my baby (on Mother's Day,
no less), as my husband pushed me in a wheelchair into the
neonatal intensive care unit. As I watched my son lying in
his incubator, surrounded by beeping monitors, with wires
attached to his scrawny preemie body, I cried so hard that my
nose bled. The Partner responded to this soggy sight with two
unforgettable lines.

One: "Whatever you do, don't get pregnant again."

More sobs; blood and mucus ooze down my lips. My husband searches for Kleenex.

Two: "Why are you so upset? You should be happy—you
almost died yesterday."

Whatever happened to the massage oil?

Om shanti.

* * *

$\mathcal{A}$ WEEK AFTER I was discharged from the hospital, while
our son was still in neonatal intensive care, I lay resting in bed
one evening when the doorbell rang. Wondering who could

be stopping by, my husband opened the door to find a couple from our former childbirthing class with their newborn.

"Hi, we're here for the class," said Minerva, the new mother. "You're hosting it tonight, aren't you?"

"Um, no, I don't think so," my husband replied.

Our teacher, Michelle, had asked Minerva and her husband, Steven, to return as the course's first proud parents, offering a grown-up show-and-tell of baby and birthing. Michelle had told them that one couple, whose wife was on bed rest, requested to have the class in their apartment. For some reason the two supposed that I was the woman confined to bed rest, although we didn't think they even knew our last names, let alone where we lived.

My husband walked them into our bedroom while telling our birthing story.

"Preeclampsia?" Minerva said nervously. "Isn't that the condition with the seizures?"

"I think it's time to go," her husband said, cringing at her description and their inopportune arrival.

"And then you can end up in a coma?" she continued.

"Yeah, that's the one," I said.

I wasn't sure whether I felt worse being reminded of the pregnancy disease or seeing their sweet infant resting peacefully in the Snugli that Minerva wore. Watching mother and new daughter, I was reminded of the hospital maternity ward, where I lay in bed with magnesium sulfate dripping into my veins to prevent seizures. I needed to be kept on that awful drug for another day after the birth. By that evening, slipping in and out of consciousness, I could no longer bear hearing happy couples with their babies in adjoining rooms, laughing with family and friends. Since leaving the hospital, we were clutching onto the daily news of our baby's weight gain in the hopes of bringing him home soon.

The four of us fell into an uncomfortable silence until the baby played her part, interrupting the pause with a loud fart. Sensing the need for a diaper change, the couple apologized again before taking off for the apartment of our friend who was on bed rest.

. . .

*T*HOSE OF US who suffer from preeclampsia pierce the myth, in Roland Barthes's words, of the "eternal lyricism of birth." We're removed from birthing rooms decorated in cheerful nursery pastels for the sterile operating room. We need IVs dispensing the potent drug magnesium sulfate, are hooked to catheters and heart monitors, and have bags of blood standing by our side in the operating room like nimble bodyguards, ready to serve on a moment's notice.

Looking back on the terrible week leading up to my hospital admittance, I realized that the midwife missed several of my warning signs of severe preeclampsia—a migraine-like headache and intense shoulder and upper abdominal pain. (As a preeclampsia specialist later told me: "The pain in your upper abdomen meant that your liver was rotting away. But don't worry—it grows back.") I've wondered whether the midwife's negligence stemmed not only from her inattentiveness and lack of medical knowledge but a blind insistence that "pregnancy is natural."

I had none of the fluid retention normally associated with

preeclampsia, just a compactly protruding eighth-month belly. Because I looked healthy and had been healthy in my frequent examinations, it was taken for granted that I would soon be participating in this eternal act of sublime suffering. Yet to assume that all women are marching toward the ninth month in glory and to focus rigidly on the supreme accomplishment of a natural birth is to be trapped in a myth that proves hollow.

"True, children are *always* born: but in the whole mass of the human problem, what does the 'essence' of this process matter to us, compared to its modes which, as for them, are perfectly historical?" wrote Barthes in his essay on the "The Family of Man" photography exhibit. "Whether or not the child is born with ease or difficulty, whether or not his birth causes suffering to his mother, whether or not he is threatened by a high mortality rate, whether or not such and such a type of future is open to him: this is what your Exhibitions should be telling people, instead of an eternal lyricism of birth."

Treating pregnancy as a healthy state rather than an illness has been a positive step of the last few decades, but progress and extremism often go hand in hand, causing blind sides and casualties. Several pregnancy ailments commonly afflict women, and the small number of us who become seriously ill can get lost in the shuffle. To be a woman over thirty-five and listen to a practitioner routinely announce that "pregnancy is natural" may seem a wondrous comfort. But the words can be a disastrous denial at a time when, according to the National Institutes of Health, reported incidents of preeclampsia jumped by 40 percent in the 1990s, in part because the disorder tends to affect older women and those carrying multiple fetuses.

. . .

*F*OLLOWING MICHAEL'S two-week hospital stay, we brought our four-pound, three-ounce little bundle home. Shortly thereafter I received a phone call from my father's niece. I was sitting in an oversized chair as the afternoon June sun tucked its plump face behind a neighboring high-rise, nursing my baby and getting acquainted with a new type of mothering—one that didn't require donning a blue robe and scrubbing my hands with a harsh orange disinfectant while my foot pushed the pedal of an industrial faucet, the neonatal intensive care unit's mechanical entrance ritual that left my skin as raw as my heart.

Tony handed me the phone, and my cousin, who is almost twice my age, offered her congratulations. Then she pointedly asked: "Didn't your dad tell you about Grandma Laurino?"

"No. What about her?"

My cousin informed me that my paternal grandmother and her oldest daughter had each lost a baby to preeclampsia. In addition, my cousin had a stillbirth at eight months, and her sister suffered full-blown eclampsia, convulsing during the delivery of her premature daughter and nearly losing her life.

"You don't know how lucky you are," said my cousin.

I held the phone in disbelief. Throughout my pregnancy, with every kick and turn in my belly, it was the inheritance of my mother upon which I mused. My dad was then eighty-two, failing in memory and unaware of the childbearing illnesses of his mother. The rest were family secrets, sad relics of nearly a half-century ago, dusted off and belatedly handed to me, the latest keeper of tradition.

During that phone call I learned about the sorrows of generations before me. At first I wondered why these stories weren't part of a communal history, one that might have fore-warned me of the dangers ahead. Shouldn't the childbearing difficulties of so many Laurino women have been acknowl-edged and collectively grieved, a way to mend and repair, a *tik-kun*, to borrow a word from Jewish tradition? But this peculiar inheritance, which turns the dream of a mystical union into a nightmare of a mother and fetus battling for nothing less than life, invites the silence of despair.

That afternoon, I was reminded again of the power of ancestry, how this life of ours curls and becomes whole like the wave. Now it had thrown me down with it, hurling me there on the beach with the well-guarded secret of generations, a shared pregnancy illness that could potentially kill the mother and cause her baby to suffocate in the womb. For all my day-dreaming about culture and metaphor, for every attempt to interpret the effects on the self of custom, tradition, and the fertile imagination of peasants who kept menstruating women away from basement wine, a more obvious fact never entered my consciousness: that my Old World inheritance was also scrawled in a genetic script determining the most fundamen-tal act, giving birth.

Mother and Child Reunion

I PREFER WRAPPING my imagination around *paesani* harvesting grapes a few hundred years back to primates hanging in trees millions of years before. Yet if I was forced to accept—in a maternity room version of at gunpoint—that the influence of my southern Italian heritage extends to genetic tendencies and complications during childbirth that may have preceded me by countless generations, what if I move the time line back much further? What role does evolutionary behavior play in the mother-child relationship?

The complications wrought by preeclampsia may well be the by-product of an evolutionary struggle between mother and child. Evolutionary biologist David Haig has spent much of his professional life pondering why pregnancy, for many women their most life-affirming act, has throughout human history also gone very wrong, causing death or debilitating illness. The conflict that could lead to preeclampsia, as Haig explained his theory in the *New York Times*, is that natural selection favors genes that allow a fetus to get more resources from the mother than the mother would necessarily like to give.

But nature should also favor mothers who can hold back these incursions and continue to reproduce. The fetus in a preeclamptic woman may be having trouble getting enough nourishment, triggering a deadly or debilitating tug-of-war as mother and unborn child engage in an unconscious struggle over these nutrients. Luckily, severe preeclampsia affects only a tiny number of us. But what about other biological realities that accord women a certain stake in the nurturing of their offspring, realities that can affect the nature of human relationships and affairs?

The evolutionary theory that presents the most difficult and enduring conflict for all women who want to combine personal ambition with motherhood has less to do with the physical act of bearing children and defined maternal roles than with the broad scope of infant needs. Almost a century after Darwin, in the late 1950s, John Bowlby, a British medical doctor and psychoanalyst, proposed his now famous insights, known as attachment theory. Bowlby asserted that infants develop into emotionally healthy human beings provided that they act upon their genetically programmed instinct to form a secure attachment with their mother or another trusted person in their first years of life.

Bowlby formed his early theories on attachment after working with emotionally unstable boys who had been separated from their mothers. He pondered crucial periods in early development and hoped to chart a course that could combine evolutionary adaptive behavior and psychoanalysis, uniting the ideas of his two scientific heroes, Darwin and Freud.

Deciding to study animals in their natural environments, Bowlby observed that when infant rhesus monkeys were separated from their mothers, they signaled distress in high-pitched calls. The longer the mother was away, the more despondent and apathetic the infant would become, clinging all the more tightly upon her return. Bowlby reasoned that infants, too, are highly sensitive actors in the evolutionary scheme, and in a fight for survival they must figure out how to protect themselves from danger. In the womb a fetus can begin to recognize the mother's voice, and shortly after birth can track her scent or be distressed by her absence.

Along with his associate, Mary Ainsworth, Bowlby would empirically test these theories on infants in a laboratory setting. Ainsworth constructed a simple twenty-minute observation called the "strange situation" test to measure an infant's response to the mother after several brief separations. She discovered that although most babies acted like Bowlby's monkeys, agitated by the mother's disappearance and quickly crawling to her upon her return, a certain number of infants responded differently. Some were agitated before the mother left but failed to be comforted by her return. A few were very angry by the short separation but refused to cuddle with the mother when she reappeared, kicking or swiping at her instead. Observing families at home and in a laboratory setting, Ainsworth saw that infants who were ambivalent or avoidant of their mother in the lab had more difficult interactions with her at home.

The "strange situation" test is still used today to record infants' attachment to their mother or primary caregiver. The studies, conducted around the world, have followed children throughout the years. The patterns remain the same: The infant who avoided the mother's eyes is more likely to ignore the teacher's instruction. Bowlby believed that family dynamics were as important as, if not more important than, genetic inheritance in producing stable, mentally healthy offspring.

Attachment theory is now considered one of the twentieth century's most influential contributions to human understanding and well-being. Bowlby's prescient charting of patterns of attachment, what he called the brain's "cognitive maps," match up to what neuroscientists are studying today; and future generations of scientists will be able to document through detailed imaging the influence of early social environments on the developing brain.

But the implications of attachment theory are troubling for any woman who seeks a place in the larger world because the theory demonstrates an infant's biological imperative that undermines, temporarily at least, the mother's autonomy. All my naive college dreams, even the idealistic Chaucerian goal of a sovereignty over self, not over others, feels irrelevant once a very needy third party enters the picture.

*   *   *

I REMEMBER the first time I questioned our child-care decisions, nervously counting on my fingers the number of hours our son spent with our part-time caregiver each week. Browsing through the morning paper, I saw an article about a study conducted by the government's National Institute of Child Health and Human Development. The study, considered to be the most comprehensive examination of child care ever undertaken in the United States, followed the development of more than a thousand children of diverse social and economic backgrounds from birth to kindergarten.

Who would have thought that Bowlby's rhesus monkeys swinging from tree to tree would influence the current debates about child care? But researchers well schooled in the literature of attachment theory, or attachment theorists themselves, raised concerns similar to those that Bowlby had touched upon decades before. The researchers reported a link between the number of hours an infant spent in "nonmaternal" care and aggressive behavior seen in the kindergarten years by teachers and mothers, as well as more teacher-child conflict.

The researchers examined all kinds of care—day care, preschool, nannies, and relatives—discovering that the more time the children had spent in any of these arrangements during their first four and a half years, the more problems and conflicts with adults would be reported. But the study also concluded that the problem behaviors were not at clinical levels of concern, and maternal sensitivity and higher family income could mitigate them, although not entirely erase them. Still, this large-scale research project, which has funding to follow children into their twenties, continues to bring forth more day-care caveats. In 2007, the National Institute released another study that found for every year a child spent at least ten hours a week in day care, regardless of the center's quality, there was a 1 percent higher score on a standardized assessment of problem behaviors compiled by teachers. According to this latest report, the problem behaviors persisted through the sixth grade.

When the first study came out in 2003, I kept reminding myself that we had hired a wonderful, nurturing woman whom we trusted more than anyone else with Michael. Yet I wondered whether that ticking clock had any hidden meaning for my son and me. I engaged in ridiculous mathematical calculations, subtracting Michael's nap time from the morning hours when Lisa, our caregiver, worked, wondering whether his sleep provided a brief reprieve from the National Institute's concerns about hours spent in "nonmaternal" care. But what if he was dreaming about Mary Poppins?

I even channeled back—as maternal guilt knows no bounds—to those two weeks and two dozen nurse mothers in the neonatal intensive care unit. Did my baby recognize Mom Number One (as opposed to Mom Number Fifteen) each time I came to visit, and not in the best of shape—still physically recuperating from my pregnancy disease and Caesarian section? My stomach twinged when I read that any infant who spent longer than seven days in the hospital was excluded from the study.

What did these potentially damaging statistics mean to all of us who must work or chose to do so? And why weren't our husbands exposed to a similar litmus test? The researchers never examined children's behavior and paternal care, which—strangely lumped into the category of "nonmaternal" care—was considered in the same league as that of the professional caregiver relationship.

I certainly wasn't alone in my reaction. Anticipating how sensitive the results of this study would be, the editors of the journal *Child Development* delayed its official publication by several months, during which they circulated the study to more than a thousand child development experts from around the world to offer a perspective on the findings or rebut them. When the journal was published—its contents were reported by every major media outlet—more troubling news appeared on its pages.

Another study, this one conducted by the University of Minnesota's Institute of Child Development, found that toddlers in day care showed a rise in the hormone cortisol compared to toddlers cared for at home. Noting that in full-day child-care centers cortisol rose in infancy, peaked in the toddler years, and decreased until no longer usually seen in early school years, the researchers theorized that interactive play in the toddler years was associated with the higher levels. (On non-child-care days, when the same children were observed at home, most showed no increases in cortisol.)

The shy children observed in the study, who probably preferred to play by themselves because they had more social fear, were found with higher levels of this hormone than children who were more adept at social play. Unlike Bowlby's monkeys, however, the higher levels of cortisol didn't appear directly related to separation distress because the rise was larger in toddlers than in infants, and seemed to be caused by the stress of social interaction. During nap time, when children weren't allowed to interact with one another, cortisol levels fell, even if the child was not asleep.

The researchers couldn't determine whether the small elevations of cortisol might have adverse effects on young children. Still they concluded: "Nonetheless, because cortisol is a potent steroid hormone that is known to affect the central nervous system, evidence that this hormone is elevated over home baseline levels for many young children in child care warrants our attention." Rising cortisol levels, child psychiatrists point out, may be associated with increased risk for "anxiety, fearfulness, depression, and lowered immune system functioning."

Of course women react defensively when findings such as these are published, which always create a flurry of media attention and bring on the silly point-counterpoint talking heads ("Jane, you ignorant day-care slut" seems more likely to be spouted on Fox News today than remembered as a Seventies *Saturday Night Live* parody). We deliver most of the care and are held to a much higher standard than our husbands. But can we rise above the din of cranky commentators telling women how to lead their lives?

Sometimes I wonder whether women find the wrong targets of ire, dismissing criticisms of day care, lashing out at attachment theory itself, or even speculating—as the editors of *Child Development* did—that children who spend very limited amounts of time in child care may be overly passive. (For Americans to worry that we're not aggressive enough is like the Japanese fretting over a lack of politeness.) Feminists seem to fear that those arbiters of family values who tell all women to stay home will gain more power by findings such as these, but that scenario seems exceedingly unlikely.

Women are major contributors to the labor pool, and a country that lives by the rules of the marketplace protects its most valuable resources. Better solutions for mothers and children can be achieved if we muster political attention and the will to help remedy this situation. But first—if equality is truly to be within reach for women—we must rid ourselves of our fictive notion of independence; we are nested in a complex, ancient, and biological system of attachments and dependencies.

Another article in *Child Development*—a staid bimonthly academic journal that became a hotbed of controversy in the summer of 2003—described a study of government-supported day-care programs in Australia. Conducted with research methods similar to those of the National Institute's, the study found no significant correlations between the quantity of "nonmaternal" day care and behavioral problems. In Australia, however, government intervention made a significant difference in the lives of working parents who are eligible for financial assistance to help pay for care. The centers have a small (five to one) child to staff ratio; and state and federal funds support child-care services from birth to age twelve, and preschool for three to five year olds. (American day care, on the other hand, understaffed and underfunded, is considered mediocre; experts say that 85 to 90 percent of the centers are below high-quality standard.) Only a small percentage of Australian families choose day care for the first year, instead using government financial assistance to help pay for informal care, such as relatives, friends, or nannies.

But Australia, with a population of only 21 million people, has been able to offer a more nurturing approach to child care, beginning with the birthing experience. An Australian journalist I know described how mothers are allowed to recuperate in the hospital for four days after giving birth, and have "a lovely little stay in which their meals are cooked for them, family can visit, and you can push your pram around." This supportive environment continues well after hospital discharge: Women go to health centers each week to get their newborns weighed, receive help with breast feeding, and, perhaps most important, become part of a community of new mothers. If, months later, a woman has trouble getting her baby to sleep through the night or is having emotional difficulties with the transition to motherhood, she can check into a private clinic with sliding-scale fees and stay for a few days to sort out her difficulties.

My Australian journalist friend gave birth to her first child in California a decade ago and was surprised by the difference in her experience compared to that of the women she knew in Australia (although she added that after years of more conservative government, Australia is paring down its resources for families, more closely imitating the American model). "So many of the women I met here were all alone with no one to help them. Everyone's family seemed to live far away and everyone's husband seemed to work incredibly long hours."

Bowlby said it was essential for mental health "that the infant and young child should experience a warm, intimate, and continuous relationship with his mother (or permanent mother substitute) in which both find satisfaction and enjoyment." If looked after by multiple caretakers early in life, the child will usually choose one with which to form a primary relationship. But children, flexible and resilient, attach to mothers, fathers, and grandparents as well as to any highly involved and skilled caregiver.

In our household, we were fortunate to have the preternaturally cheerful Lisa, who was as deeply involved as Tony and I were in the minutia of Michael's daily habits. Lisa and I were the frontline-attachment women during those early days, a time that I found isolating and lonely. With Lisa leaving by midafternoon, I'd search for any organized activities that Michael and I could attend, but all the classes in my neighborhood were offered only in the morning. At the time, my vision of nirvana was an afternoon session of Gymboree.

. . .

MOTHERS ATTACHED to their children; children attached to their mothers. Who could read this literature and not wonder about his or her own place in the family scheme when the mother's loving eyes meet the child's inchoate gaze? John Bowlby, the father of attachment theory, had a lifelong preoccupation with his intellectual hero, Charles Darwin, and devoted the last years of his life to a psychiatric case study of the evolutionist. Darwin's lifelong array of debilitating physical and psychological ills, theorized Bowlby, was tied to the trauma that the young Darwin experienced after his mother died and he was left to be raised by an emotionally distant father and imperious sisters. More recent biographers have turned a similarly close eye to the upbringing of Bowlby himself, who was raised in an upper-class British family. Bowlby's primary attachment was to his governess, and he was devastated by her departure from the family when he was four years old.

All cultures share similarities, but each approaches nurturing children with its own singular biases and traditions. When Bowlby described a study of two- and three-year-old children who were reluctant to attend a playdate without being accompanied by their mother (he was making the point that four and five year olds cling less), he noted that the children "were all from skilled artisan and professional white families and came mostly of old

American stock. Their upbringing had tended to be conservative and strict. They had not, therefore, been mollycoddled."

Genetically and culturally, I'm from that mollycoddled stock, doted and fussed upon by Italian mothers and aunts. My upbringing was not particularly strict other than my parents insisting that I attend church and Sunday school each week; in fact, the needs of the young child surpassed that of the parent, so I had no imposed early bedtime and was never disciplined by spanking, the common practice of the day.

But the culture of the mamma, headquartered in the kitchen and sadly restricting the gifts of women to one dimension of life, would simply get too hot, multiple burners glowing simultaneously in that small, often oppressive space of maternal devotion. At times, as I watched the steam escape from the lids of those boiling pots, it seemed as though the water was mimicking my self-consciousness: Add the heat of an overbearing love, and identity turns to vapor, dissipates.

Yet years later, I would discover another of water's permutations: Add the chill of a brittle self-involvement, and the spirit turns to ice.

"I saw a bad movie once with one good line," I overheard one mother tell another, urging the woman not to worry about how her extensive work overseas was affecting the mood and behavior of her young son at home. "Your child would rather have you committing suicide in the next room than fulfilling your desires."

That bad movie line, good enough for the woman to repeat, is packed with a hostility toward family responsibilities that has shadowed feminism for decades. A young child's desire to be with his parents as much as possible, or his wish that mom or dad would wipe his nose, is not a purposeful oppression of individual freedom; it is the sometimes frustrating and tiring but also inspiring and joy-filled reality of attachment and dependency, otherwise known as family life.

Now, as a mamma myself with a ten-year-old son (who knows how to make me a delicious cup of espresso), I often feel as though the quest for autonomy has gone awry. If we accept that children's finely attuned biological needs influence their ability to be caring and nurturing adults, then as scholar Jean Bethke Elstain argued in her book *Public Man, Private Woman*, it is the public sphere, not the private world, that "should be the target of the social rebel and feminist critic."

Contemporary feminists have long agreed that a more just society for women and children must first include our partners playing a key role in caregiving, and it necessitates an adjustment of resources so more money is spent on early child care than on prisons, and that tax dollars provide universal health care, not bigger bombs. But the movement's primary objective, taking on the enormous challenge of helping women achieve personal autonomy and economic equality—tackling in a few decades several centuries' worth of social and political bias—made it reluctant to bring women's concerns as wives and mothers to the top of the political agenda.

At first this decision seemed a rational, tactical one—the feminist movement held a vision of a rational world in which women's goals were compatible with one another (or would be after sufficient consciousness raising), and values like social equality could be achieved after women joined men in the workforce. But today's political climate, combined with feminists' continued ambivalence about the importance of parents spending time with their children (instead of paid child care), has precluded any coherent national campaign against the economic and social realities that impede women's ability to nurture and to work.

Two decades ago, Americans and Europeans worked roughly the same number of hours each year. As the pace of modernity accelerated, ensuring that work and pleasure can rarely coexist, American men and women now labor a daunting four hundred hours a year more than Europeans. Time's innumerable and irreplaceable pleasures—the poetry unfurled in a spare hour or two replaced by the prosaic notion of "quality time"—have been steadily stripped from family life.

Feminism's rationalism dovetailed perfectly with capitalism's creed. But rationalism, the philosopher's tool, proved a curse to poets, and life calls for more poetry than reason when responding to a child's needs.

A mother will experience a time in the waning hours of a summer afternoon when a cloud bursts and her rain-drenched child, shivering in the back of an air-conditioned bus, beseeches her to make the goose bumps go away. In that shimmering, ephemeral moment in which she cuddles her child, she will sense, however briefly, a ray of meaning in the arbitrariness of the day. The child, warmed by his mother, continues to play, turning from her to climb and peer out his window seat. And the empty-armed mother recalls a feeling she had first intuited after giving birth—that the infant's determined reach and child's imploring eyes retell our most primal tale of separation, longing, and the essential human need to secure a steady place.

Fertile Feminism

In which we move toward
a new feminist paradigm

$\mathcal{N}$IDIA, A WORKING-CLASS mother of three, knows what it's like to raise a family without paid leave, without part- or flex-time options, and with only two weeks of vacation a year. I met Nidia through my friend Joanna, who teaches at the City University Center for Worker Education, an adult college degree program in which Nidia was enrolled.

Nidia, whose family came from Puerto Rico, grew up and raised her children, now twenty-seven, twenty-one, and seventeen, on the Lower East Side of Manhattan. To say that she is bitter about her work experience while trying to raise a family cannot fully capture the mixture of anger and regret that was revealed in her monotone and sometimes sarcastic responses to my questions.

"I always had to work. I barely spent any time with my

children. With my middle child, I went back to work two days after he was born," she told me. At the time, Nidia was a data processor for a vocational school, and her husband worked in security for a bank. "I didn't get to bond with any of them." But she had no choice; she and her husband needed her income, and if she didn't go back to work right away, her company would replace her.

The most time Nidia had off was the three and a half months she spent at home after her first son was born, a result of being temporarily unemployed. Not so with her daughter. Nidia returned to work shortly after her birth. "We never bonded—it was babysitter to day care to preschool. When you finally get to spend time with them, you don't even know them, especially the middle child."

Nidia had the most trouble with her middle child, who stopped attending high school, a fact that she and her husband learned from a truancy officer. Nidia felt judged and belittled when she and her husband found out about her son's behavior, even though she felt obliged to return to work two days after her son was born; even though throughout the years she could take only one week of her ten days of paid vacation at a time, and rarely during school holidays because she was too low on the office totem pole for this prized time slot; even though she wasn't allowed to use the phone at work and had to sneak in calls to see whether her children had arrived home safely from school. "If the child gets out of hand," she told me, "[the school is] the first to blame you. But they don't let you set the values or standards."

After discovering the truancy problem, Nidia, tired of a New World reasoning that told her to work long hours away from home while raising a family, decided to take things into her own hands "the old-fashioned way," as she described it. She took a week off, not caring what her employer thought. She locked the doors and window gates, and sat inside the house with her son, refusing to budge. It was a rough week, she told me, with her son even breaking a window in a rage against his mother. But Nidia wouldn't relent; she told him that this was his future, trapped inside with her if he didn't straighten out. And eventually he did, says Nidia, earning a high school equivalency degree and enrolling in a community college, where today he is studying to be a paramedic. "Now he thanks me."

As Nidia was telling me her story, and I saw the resentment of a woman close to my age but with such a vastly different life experience, I felt embarrassed to ask the next question: Did she consider herself a feminist or at any time support the movement?

"Let me see," she replied with a sly smile, "is that when women fought for the right to employment?"

With her children now grown, Nidia believes that "it would have made a big difference in their lives and mine" if she had been able to spend more time with them. "They had to do everything early—maintain our apartment, feed themselves. If they need to survive on their own, they will, but as far as closeness and a relationship, I don't think we bonded in that way."

Although it would be comforting to think that Nidia's story is a relic of an Eighties workforce, the problems she encountered—lack of benefits, minimal vacation time, no flexibility, even the inability to use an office phone to call home—are the same issues that researchers cite today when documenting the difficulties faced by working-class parents.

Luli, a single mother of a three and a four year old, broke down crying as she told me her story. Her mother had helped care for her children; but after her mother fell ill, Luli's life became a scramble to keep a job (she was unemployed when we met, having been fired from two jobs in the past few years), try to earn her college degree, and take care of her children. At a shoe company in which Luli performed accounting and secretarial work, she asked to change her schedule for a week in order to visit several day-care centers near her home. Luli wanted to take her lunch hour at the end of the day, allowing her to leave at five instead of six, so that she could observe the centers before they closed. "They weren't very supportive, and in fact let me go," Luli explained, as the company found her complicated life too difficult for their needs.

In the report "One Sick Child Away from Being Fired," Joan Williams, who heads the Work Life Law Center at the University of California's Hastings College of the Law, compiled ninety-nine union arbitration cases that detailed how blue- and pink-collar workers are being fired for simply acting like parents, such as deciding to leave early to pick up a sick child from school. The report described how the job demands in today's unfettered marketplace are plaguing the lives of working-class parents and putting their children in jeopardy. In one case, a woman janitor of twenty-seven years was dismissed after failing to come to work on a Saturday afternoon. The mother of a severely mentally retarded seventeen-year-old son, she had to stay home because his caregiver had suddenly become ill. Luckily for this woman, an arbitrator reinstated her in the job, although—of all such cases examined—employers won more often than employees. At least these workers had union protection and representation, unlike—as Williams points out—the other 92 percent of Americans employed by the private sector.

. . .

𝓘F CONTEMPORARY feminism helped contribute to the quandary in which we're currently stuck—rationally addressing the problem of economic equality by devaluing the act of care and asking women to perform in the workforce just like men—it will be feminism that lifts us out of these muddy waters. Women must bring new ideas to the public arena with a loud, clear, unified voice. It will take a grassroots effort, similar in scope to the one that conservatives have waged over the past few decades, to educate Americans that caring for children is part of the fabric of civic life, and government has an essential role to play in aiding women's ability to work while protecting the need to nurture.

For college girls who never heard the word "feminism" mentioned in a conversation or have no idea of what it means, they should listen to—before they become mothers—some women whom I'd certainly choose, if such a vote could be had, to help change public policy in America today: lawyer Joan Williams, philosopher Eva Feder Kittay, and pediatrician and public policy specialist Jody Heymann. These women, three of many erudite voices on this subject, have rethought the feminist agenda of the past forty years, brilliantly analyzed the inherent contradictions of equality and dependency, and proposed much-needed reforms. As Heymann has argued, workplace reforms can't be left solely to the marketplace because businesses do not have enough financial incentives to make the necessary changes, no matter how much these actions would benefit all of society.

Helping rectify the inevitable conflict between equality and dependency is clearly an issue of social justice, but the words "justice" and "fairness" fall on deaf ears in America today. More palatable to lawmakers is that it's in the country's economic interest to finally address this issue. As the balance between work and family is being pushed to the point of breaking, women's participation in the workforce has been declining. Whereas in 1997, nearly 60 percent of married mothers with infants were in the labor force, today the number has fallen to 53 percent, and a similar, if slightly smaller, decline exists among married mothers of preschool children (60 percent compared to 64 percent ten years ago). The White House Council of Economic Advisors, in a report presented to Congress in 2006, cautioned that the leveling off of women in the workforce was affecting the country's potential for economic growth. "Diminishing economic growth potential" are key words to rouse somnambulant political leaders.

Jody Heymann's Project on Global Working Families created an index of needed reforms, which is one place to start a national dialogue and set a policy agenda. The index includes paid leave for childbearing; affordable and accessible high-quality child care for the first three years of life; high-quality early childhood education for three to five year olds; educational opportunities and supervision for school-age children throughout the year; paid leave to all working adults when they need to attend to their child's educational or developmental needs; and paid leave and flexibility for children's health needs.

Kittay has formed a sophisticated political theory around the simple truth that everyone is "some mother's child," instructing us toward a philosophy that supports an ethic of care and helps to fulfill the societal obligation "to attend to relationships upon which all civic relationships depend."

And Williams argues for a "reconstructive feminism," or what she also calls "family humanism," seeking to build social coalitions around the goal of redefining a workplace in which women and men can better split the caregiving responsibilities, and one in which parents are not marginalized for working less. For professional women, "the key issue is not whether employers have flexible policies on their books, but whether the policies provided break the traditional link between flexibility and marginalization," writes Williams in *Unbending Gender*.

Williams imagines a society in which men and women are working together for the same cause: a restructured workforce. She proposes that part-time workers receive proportional rates of pay, benefits, and advancement; and she suggests that men and women could better share the child-rearing responsibilities and spend more time with their young children by each working a four-day week, alternating their day off. Such a schedule would enable children to be cared for by their parents for two days of the workweek and professional child care for the other three. "Given the level of anger that exists in many American households over the issue of family work," writes Williams, "the desire of many fathers to spend more time with their children, and a social context where the father would not suffer catastrophic career consequences for his part-time commitment, many fathers might just agree."

• • •

$\mathcal{M}$Y HUSBAND eventually found a new work schedule that allowed him to spend more time with Michael and better share the child-rearing responsibilities. I wish I could say that we had planned this job switch rather than having stumbled upon it. I had always hoped Tony could work fewer hours—especially in the first few years when caregiving was the most difficult—but his job in government had much less flexibility than my writing schedule, and his earnings, not mine, paid the rent.

The notion of sharing economic equality with my husband had ended years before we had a child. After Dinkins lost the mayoralty and I my job, I decided not to look for work in the well-paying field of speechwriting, wanting to return instead to freelance journalism and book writing. Our income shrunk significantly, but Tony, who grew up hearing the click of typewriter keys in his household—his father is a nonfiction writer and novelist who left his more lucrative job in advertising the moment he could possibly afford to—supported and encouraged my decision. Not that I enjoy being poorly compensated for my work, but I am grateful to be able to pursue this work while my husband's job provides health and pension benefits.

We could afford part-time child care, so when Michael was four months old I returned to my work, reducing the number of hours I wrote each day and splitting the caregiving responsibilities with Lisa. I left the house in the morning and returned by half past one so Lisa had enough time to travel to her neighborhood, an hour away, to pick up her own son, who had just started kindergarten. The relationship worked extremely well because it served the desires of two women: The morning hours gave me the time I needed to finish writing a book, and Lisa, a member of a close-knit Trinidadian family who helped support one another, also wanted part-time work while her son was young. When I asked Lisa whether she could work longer hours two days a week, one of her sisters pitched in to pick up Lisa's son.

I remember coming home every afternoon to greet Michael in his crib, join him in playing with the colorful mobile, and make silly faces to my giggling boy. It was utterly delightful—until I looked at the clock to see that only ten minutes had passed. What in the world was I going to do to entertain him until Tony got home at seven?

It was during those hours that I realized an essential problem with nurturing in a country that rewards individualism, doesn't value care, and offers little community support for mothers and children. For decades women were told that the traditional role of the primary breadwinner entailed a sacrifice equal to that of staying home with children. But how can the sacrifice be similar when the professional male's identity is largely defined by his work? Despite the financial pressures that this role entails, any woman who thrives on an intellectual and social engagement with the world understands the loss that she'll experience in order to nurture the dependent child. The work can feel particularly oppressive, as Eva Feder Kittay observed, "because the norm of freedom is shaped without attention to the role of dependency in our lives."

When I was pregnant, I remember watching a video in my doctor's office about breast feeding while a nurse monitored my glucose tolerance. A woman on the tape described motherhood as "the hardest job I've ever had," and I condescendingly thought, This woman has obviously never had the kinds of jobs I've had. I knew the meaning of a fourteen-hour workday and the need to produce under deadline pressure. I recalled a mayoral trip to Japan in 1993 when the phone rang in my hotel room in the middle of the night informing me that the World Trade Center had been bombed for the first time. Groggy and trying to process the news, I was told I had less than half an hour to write a statement for the mayor to read on a television feed beamed to New York.

I didn't know, however, that nurturing a newborn was a relentless twenty-four-hour-a-day job, performed despite a lack of sleep. Caring for my son, especially in the infant and toddler years, was far more difficult than the demanding jobs I once held because the ways in which my mind had been trained were of little use in my new role. Why did I go to graduate school? I'd wonder during afternoons of watching the mobile sway above the crib, chasing garbage trucks down the street, and stuffing soiled diapers into the tidy Diaper Genie. And why didn't I invent the Diaper Genie?

The possibility to change Tony's schedule arrived in the form of an irresistible offer: a one-year position as a visiting professor, teaching graduate students urban economic development, crisis management, and education—all areas in which he had worked in government. It was a pleasant year for the three of us. During the days when Tony didn't teach, as the light of the late afternoon sun reached our living room, father and son could head to the park to play catch. For once we didn't feel like time's harried casualties, and we took a four-week summer vacation. When the academic year ended, Tony was determined to maintain a more flexible schedule while Michael was young.

Tony had two job offers—to continue teaching at the university and head a research center there, or to take a top administrative position at another university. The latter position paid more than twice the salary of the teaching job but demanded many more hours. Tony knew he could decrease the salary gap with some consulting work, but the difference was sizable. Still, both of us believed that the teaching position best suited our family's needs.

What surprised me, however, was the reaction of my husband's friends and colleagues. Although I couldn't hide my delight that one of us had a steady paycheck plus flexibility, none of his friends could believe that he turned down the higher paying, more powerful job. It was a "no-brainer" to take the administrative position, a former colleague told him. For a man to give up day-to-day power and more money to spend time with his family is still looked upon with suspicion and disbelief. That infamous line—"He wanted to spend more time with his family"—appearing in newspaper stories in which a prominent man suddenly leaves his job has become synonymous with a nod, a wink, and oh well he got canned.

. . .

$\mathcal{P}$ART OF the problem, of course, is that we live in an era in which sacrificing a goal, even temporarily, seems an affront to our heritage and ingrained perceptions of freedom. A consumer culture sells happiness as the product of abundant choices; it cannot accommodate the humbler belief that happiness may be closer to our reach by more graciously accepting the measure of loss in each choice we make.

To publicly suggest that women are faced with competing truths and incompatible goals can mean paying dearly for your words, as it did for Joyce Purnick, a reporter and former Metro editor at the *New York Times*. A few years back, Purnick gave the commencement address at her alma mater, Barnard College, during which she speculated that she wouldn't have broken the gender barrier to become the first female Metro editor of the *New York Times* if she had been raising a young child. The job required, she explained, working twelve-hour days, sometimes seven days a week. Purnick argued, and also regretted, that one of the ways in which she had made herself competitive was by sacrificing a personal life, until she married at forty-two, to devote herself to the *Times*. "You *cannot* have it all," she told the new graduates. "Having it all is a phrase for books and speeches by political leaders."

At several points in her speech, Purnick defended the institution's demands rather than pondering how society can better respond to the reality of parents' needs. For example, she said it wouldn't be fair for those who took time off to raise children to be promoted above someone who worked long days and rarely took vacations. Purnick had spent her career fulfilling what Joan Williams calls the norm of the "ideal worker," an impossible standard for most women because it is framed around men's bodies and asks the employee to work full time, overtime, and take little or no leave for child rearing. Purnick didn't seem to consider how parents who take time off to nurture can lend a needed humanism to bureaucracies; and she was a bit Pollyannaish about merit promotions in large institutions. A selfless, dedicated, and hardworking employee should be compensated for her achievements, but unfortunately a smooth-talking sycophant can get there first.

But it was Purnick's declaration that in all choice there is loss, that you can't have it all, that most infuriated people. (Members of the women's studies department considered walking out of the commencement address.) Wire services quickly picked up this theme, reporting it here and abroad: "Women's hard-won equality in the workplace suffered a blow in the United States," read the Manchester *Guardian*, "after a woman editor at the *New York Times* sparked a national debate."

"I was appalled," responded Jill Hamburg, associate editor of *Working Woman* magazine. "It was so ironic. She makes [her comments] on the day that Jill Barad, the chief executive of Mattel, appears on the cover of *BusinessWeek*. She has two children."

Purnick never said that work and motherhood were incompatible, hypothesizing that if she were raising a child, "I'd be a reporter, or a lower-level editor. I might even be happier." What Purnick said was that a job that required twelve-hour days, sometimes seven days a week, precluded the necessary time for nurturing. Most women agree; studies show that 95 percent of mothers aged twenty-five to forty-four work less than fifty hours a week. But Purnick was publicly and privately pilloried for stating that certain choices preclude making other choices, a truth inherent in any life.

* * *

$\mathscr{D}$URING THE YEARS when Tony was teaching, he met someone on a consulting project who asked whether he'd be interested in becoming a policy advisor to then-gubernatorial candidate Eliot Spitzer. Tony's academic schedule enabled him to sign on, and when Spitzer was elected governor he asked Tony to head a major agency. Yes, those relaxed hours disappeared, and I missed that extra time together tremendously, but men, too, must have faith that temporarily stepping back during the early child-rearing years doesn't mean removing themselves from work in which they thrive.

For it is this group—highly educated professionals with the most bargaining power and flexibility—that can begin to reshape the roles of fathers and mothers by choosing or insisting upon different work schedules, especially when their children are infants and toddlers. Several years ago, in a cover story for the *New York Times* Sunday magazine, reporter Lisa Belkin argued that we were witnessing the beginning of a new "revolution"—highly educated women married to financially successful men were choosing to temporarily (they hoped, but of course had no guarantee) drop out of the workplace to raise their children. Belkin had interviewed a number of women, many of whom had completed postgraduate work, who found that the overwhelming demands of a sixty-hour-plus workweek left them physically and emotionally depleted, and they decided to leave jobs that deprived them of time to raise their children. Many of the younger women interviewed for the article never entered the workforce after completing years of postgraduate work, confident that raising children should initially be their sole priority.

Belkin theorized that if women continued to pursue less demanding jobs, or decided not to work while their children were young, more men would eventually follow their humane lead and reevaluate the culture of the workplace and their role as fathers. Although I wanted to share Belkin's optimism about the possibility of a cultural shift that placed a higher value on nurturing—especially having seen my husband's evolving ideas about the role of fathers and the constraints of the workplace—it was hard for me to believe that the individual actions of economically privileged women constituted a social revolution. I also wondered whether these women had made a fair bargain with themselves, assuming that they could find work down the road at a time when the marketplace has become brutally competitive and no powerful organization exists to advocate for women's needs as mothers and workers.

But even in its best case scenario, this "revolution" would affect only a fraction of the workforce—highly educated, upper-middle-class professionals in stable marriages. Nidia and Luli taught me that if you walk into a room of working-class people and ask them how they are getting by, you are more likely to see anger or tears than discover the beginnings of a social revolution around the issue of childcare. Many women have little or no ability to take leave time or reduce their work schedules, and the social and political beliefs of contemporary society, deeply invested in the power of the individual and skeptical of government's role in providing equity, reinforces this untenable situation.

· · ·

$\mathcal{S}$OME WOMEN SCHOLARS argue that feminism wasn't always as disconnected from the private realm as it is today but diverged in that direction in the twentieth century and never returned to its more complicated roots. Janet Giele's *Two Paths to Women's Equality: Temperance, Suffrage, and the Origins of Modern Feminism* examines both movements and offers a broader picture of temperance women than the rigid, puritanical teetotaler. Many temperance leaders took up their crusade because of the profound loss of a husband or a son to alcohol abuse, channeling their grief into creating what they believed was a better society.

They developed, argues Giele, "an ideology that linked women's power in the home to their power in the public sphere . . . By building on the woman's temperance crusade and wrapping themselves in the symbols and language of churches, women's temperance advocates subtly expanded the feminine role from hearth to public arena." The suffragettes, on the other hand, acted more like the precursors to the modern feminist movement, focusing on women's equality.

Giele suggests that mainstream feminism would be well served by adopting strategies similar to those of moderate temperance leaders, who also supported the suffrage movement and convinced homemakers of the importance of achieving the vote. Yet protecting the health of their families was the primary concern of temperance leaders, which led them to fight for causes such as the purification of drinking water. The impasse and lack of broader support toward the feminist movement today, writes Giele, will never be rectified unless these two strands of the women's movement—one that sought to protect women's interest as wives and mothers, the other that fought for universal human rights—converge once again.

A feminist motherhood agenda: To modern ears, the words ring of contradictions. If, generally speaking, feminism engages us in the world, motherhood, at least temporarily, draws us away. Feminism looks outward—a bold attempt to change the values of a society in which men hold most positions of power and decision making; motherhood turns instinctively inward, fiercely geared toward protecting your child. Crossing the street is an act of new vigilance; telling the truth about the world means delving full force into matters of innocence and denial.

With the traumatic events of the past few years, this disconnect between public and private has often felt like a chronic, throbbing ache. As my eyes glance at the morning paper, successive days melding into years, I've been asked to comprehend the incomprehensible: the Twin Towers inferno in downtown Manhattan that rose two miles from where we live; the person with the entrepreneurial idea to produce a lethal form of biological warfare and disperse death with a postage stamp; the shock and awe of an Iraqi war; the Madrid and London bombings; the recognition of war's destruction from a lie spun out of control.

I'd pop a waffle into the toaster for my son as the "Arthur" theme song filled the room, my eyes embarrassingly made teary by Ziggy Marley's lilting Caribbean rhythms ("I say hey, what a wonderful kind of day / if we can learn to work and play / and get along with each other"). Holding a knife, my hand carefully and rhythmically spreads the slowly melting butter, as if covering the waffle's every crevice could offer a protective glaze.

I look up and see my son giggling with the cartoon characters, savoring each sip of his favorite juice. On some days, it's been a struggle to walk out the door. The reflex to protect is biological, emotional, rewriting the fairy tale to erase the prickly forests and raging seas hindering the path to a happy ever after. It is my mother's hand brushing her sixty-one-year-old-son's hair; it is my voice making up stories with mischievous animals but no bad men. It is the reflex to stay inside when the outside world overwhelms. The opposite of paving the way for social change.

Yet eventually we have to leave the house, and so do our children.

The women who are dropping out of, or never entering, the workforce because they can afford to will be sorely missed in an environment that needs the sensibilities of employees with a strong instinct to nurture. These women may also become frustrated abandoning their ambitions because they can't find flexible work hours to spend long days at home caring for their infants and young children. If we are truly to experience the social revolution that Belkin described, then change can start with these women with law, business, and doctoral degrees who understand firsthand both the demands of the workforce and the cries of their children. They can become the grassroots leaders of a reinvigorated, refocused women's movement.

To borrow Thomas S. Kuhn's famous phrase about the process of scientific discovery, feminism is in need of a paradigm shift—a new way of thinking about a once revolutionary model that became trapped in its own limitations, hobbling along for years, bound to the framework it created but desperately demanding a vision to replace it.

"Though the world does not change with a change of paradigm," wrote Kuhn, "the scientist afterward works in a different world." What an extraordinary idea—that once we accept a change from the previous model, our view of the world and place within it changes too. Applying Kuhn's scientific metaphor to the social sciences offers the tantalizing proposition to shape our lives differently through individual and collective acts.

By hiring help or forming collective arrangements such as babysitting co-ops to enable stay-at-home mothers to carve out some quiet hours each day, those seeking to reenter the workforce can begin to imagine and configure a role for themselves and their husbands in an alternative work environment. By meeting in coffee shops, creating blogs, or joining already existing groups, these women can articulate their needs before sharing this vision with political and business leaders.

Combining the temperance leaders' quest for social justice and the suffragettes' passion for universal human rights, a new feminist model must assert a societal vision that rejects the overwhelming demands of the workplace and proposes specific reforms. It needs to shift from a model of personal and economic equality, predicated on the need for autonomy, to a more inclusive vision: family connectedness and economic sustainability, predicated on the need for interdependence. Insisting, like the temperance leaders before them, that women's interests as mothers must be protected, a new vision of feminism can help bridge the movement's historical chasm between elite professionals and the clock-punching employees.

But there's one big difference from the temperance move-ment. Embrace those barrels of basement wine! Women need to tap the potential of Old World truths that sit before us corked and untouched, waiting for a new way to pour forth, like the afternoon treat that my cousin once siphoned into his Royal Crown soda bottle. Women need ample space for human relationships; a willingness to sacrifice a piece of their desires to care for another; a trust in intuition as well as rea-son; a belief in life's essence as private not public; a deeply rooted connection to family—*in vino veritas*.

Today, I can no longer dismiss as dusty old relics cultural values that sought to protect the sanctity of the family. I've come to imagine that the Old World's deeply ingrained famil-ial instincts can serve as a backdrop to a broader discussion about care: Who is going to provide it and who is going to help pay for it? Perhaps the nature of being an "in-between" per-son, those of us who straddle the competing and conflicting values of our hyphenated ancestries, means resisting cultural extremes, searching instead for a place that, at least in the imagination, melds what's worth preserving with life-affirming change. Which leads me to believe that the granddaughters and great-granddaughters of immigrants, using the New World tools of education and its principles of justice, can help fash-ion a society that will not undermine our ability to work and to nurture but significantly aid it.

I'm not suggesting a nostalgic surrender to a falsely imag-ined better time, but rather a wider, more inclusive lens in which women and men can view the world. Despite the demands of our anxious, computerized lives and our inbred drive to compete, when we nurture we come closest to imitating the quality of mind that peasants inherited as their birthright—the Old World's reliance on mystery and devotion, its measuring life by the rhythm of the seasons.

The mother who temporarily abandons the public world's obsession with appearances, dreamily breast feeding her baby, joyfully dancing in the snow, purposefully sculpting with Play-Doh, intuitively adopts the quality of mind that Romantic poet John Keats believed necessary in forming a "Man of Achievement." "That is," Keats wrote to his brothers, "when man is capable of being in uncertainties, mysteries, doubts, without any irritable reaching after fact and reason." Keats called it negative capability and thought that Shakespeare possessed it in enormity. Imagine the gifts that would unfold in the lives of men, the essential humanity that would come to light, if they spent more than just a few weekend hours cuddling, playing with, feeding, and rocking to sleep their infants.

In recent years, Americans have enthusiastically embraced elements of Old World culture in our daily lives, except we don't use the words "Old World" but more fashionable terms like "organic," "local," and "artisanal" (derived from the Italian *artigiano*). In a one-hour PBS special on Alice Waters, the chef of Chez Panisse, food writers and social critics described the revolution she created—one with roots, viewers were told, in the peace and feminist movements in Berkeley.

Waters's "revolution," inspired, she explained, by how the French shop daily at small markets, was to reject the mass production of food. Ruby red raspberries picked on a nearby farm in the morning would be served on dessert plates that evening at the lovely Chez Panisse. A by-product of the astounding level of affluence in American society today has been the transformation of the word "revolution," now rendered practically meaningless in the sense of radically changing the established social and economic structure of society. It's become a revolution for upper-middle-class professional women to opt to stay home with their children and have dinner with their husbands at Chez Panisse.

But if we grant Waters her revolution, how, other than in scale, is the decision to buy locally produced food (and to respect food and the people who produce it, as Waters has said) any different from my grandmother each morning entering the garden that my grandfather cultivated to select the tomatoes, zucchini, and eggplant that she would prepare for dinner that night? The American fascination with wine, from harvesting to fermenting and tasting grapes, stems from this same inclination—and a sense that not all of modernity is healthy or pleasing to the senses.

Even the Old World practice of making wine has reemerged in the new millennium, this time exclusively packaged. A California wine "country club," according to the *New York Times*, charges a $140,000 initiation fee for the privilege of harvesting several rows of Napa grapes. Among the club's members is a doctor from my hometown who describes the delight of having his "fingers soaked in grape juice" and boards a jet to California to seek a wine finer than what he makes in his refrigerated garage in Short Hills, New Jersey. While I once flew from the idea of my grandfathers crushing grapes, now we're told—if we're wealthy enough to afford it—to slow down and smell the full bouquet.

Because we've lost faith in society's ability to act collectively, people are hoping that their individual choices can
make a difference. Mothers are buying organic to protect
their children's health, rejecting processed foods and supporting local farmers. But their actions are, of course, merely
the tip of the mesclun in dealing with the damage done in
the last few decades by the monumental increase in private
profits over the public interest. Strengthening the rights of
working parents is a struggle no doubt harder to achieve than
rejecting mass production by buying organic, but it is one
whose rewards, if true political changes were made, would
be innumerable.

Once women agree on a vision for a national feminist
movement that makes care its core principle, more creative
solutions to help working parents will abound, such as the
proposal put forth by Germany's new family affairs minister.
Although eager to pare down her country's extensive existing
benefits of three years' paid leave (and responding to German
women's concerns that this lengthy time off has marginalized them in the workforce), she initiated a twelve-month
paid-leave program of up to $2,500 a month, or fourteen
months if mother and father share the leave time. Successful
government-financed day-care programs in France and Australia are models waiting to be imitated.

Universal pre-K classes for three- and four-year-olds have
proven to be one of the most valuable indicators of later academic success, and a national program is needed to fund and
build these schools. Such a program can take lessons—as
many early childhood educators already have done—from
the culture of the mamma. Reggio Emilia, a small town in

northern Italy, is the birthplace of one of the most highly respected preschool education systems in the world.

The government must also help ensure that a rich variety of after-school programs exists for elementary school children. A domestic version of the Peace Corps—call it the Care Corps—could be created, employing college students to supervise after-school clubs, sports programs, and summer camps; senior citizens could be enlisted to help watch preschoolers.

California, Washington, and New Jersey now offer the only paid-leave programs in the country. These programs, taking advantage of the states' temporary disability benefits, offer creative possibilities for putting together family leave insurance. In New Jersey employees can contribute less than one dollar a week, taken from their earnings, into a family leave fund. The contributions provide New Jersey workers with two-thirds of their usual wages, up to a maximum of $524 a week for six weeks, enabling them to take time off after the birth of a child or to care for a sick family member. Although the proposal costs businesses nothing, and in fact makes small firms more competitive by offering a benefit that larger corporations can better afford, the New Jersey business community, including the Association of Women Business Owners, opposed the original legislation, arguing that hiring temporary employees is too costly.

Legislation such as this helps low-income workers most; women employed by large corporations are usually able to combine company benefits and vacation time to take three months of paid leave after the birth of a child. With so little in place and so much more that is needed, only a nationally powerful group of women can begin to change the social landscape. It should be the type of organization that can command millions to march on Washington to protect a woman's right to choose, and it must effectively advocate for a national policy of paid parental leave, arguing that American productivity will be weakened if women continue to leave the workforce. Jody Heymann points out that government paid leave is provided in 165 countries, *even sub-Saharan Africa*, with only Estonia and Colombia faring worse than the United States in this tiny coalition of the unwilling.

Republicans profess family values but have offered empty rhetoric. The American Dream Restoration Act in the Contract with America included a $500 tax credit for each child, capped at two children and excluding couples who earn more than $130,000 a year. The government must offer much bolder solutions. The fact that Republicans, not Democrats, came up with the initial idea for a child tax credit is indicative of how deeply divided progressive women have been about tackling the child-care problem, fearing a life back at home baking cookies. Compensation for dependency work is a means to bridge the gap between a promise of equality and the reality of dependency. By working within the already existing structure of the American tax code, the credit should be raised to $10,000—an amount that can impact the lives of the working and middle class.

To offer parents a $10,000 tax credit until a child reaches three years of age would allow women more meaningful choices; they could continue working and put the money toward paying for higher quality child care or stay home and be partially compensated for dependency work. It would give couples better financial options to temporarily pare down their schedules and work part-time during those critical early years of attachment. And it would cost substantially less than the Iraq War. Unlike the futile but well-meaning Wages for Housework campaign launched by feminists decades ago, a tax credit not only supports the needs of women but recognizes the biological and social realities that children need early, steady nurturing.

And why should we do this? The former speechwriter in me can write that well-nurtured children will become reliable, emotionally stable future citizens and members of a productive, energetic, and creative workforce. The descendant of Uncle Patsy in me will write: If you don't want somebody else's kid settling an argument with yours with a knife or a gun, pay some attention to this issue.

Is this just another tax and spend idea that throws money at problems? Well, here I'll quote my husband, who did take that teaching position at Princeton. This is what he told his graduate students: Budgets are about choices. Choices are about values.

What are our values? How can government help meet our ideals, goals, and aims? What role do citizens have to play in determining where we allocate our resources?

Because employees have so little protection, the work-family conflict is being addressed today American style: A growing number of people who have been fired from their jobs after taking time off to care for a needy infant or a parent are taking legal action, and in several cases are awarded sizable sums by sympathetic juries. These large sums will no doubt put employers on guard, but lawsuits are a narrow way to tackle social policy issues. As Joan Williams told the *New York Times*, lawsuits "are the worst possible vehicle for social change, except for nothing, and that's where we are right now. . . . What's happening in public policy in this arena? It took more than a decade to pass the Family and Medical Leave Act, and it's very limited. So when people say, 'Well, the lawsuits are limited achievements,' I say, 'Well, compared to what? You're not in Europe.' "

Yet if women could collectively manage to ban a national pastime like consuming alcohol, can't we raise our glasses today to forging a creative and determined political effort to address this issue? As much as I long for an Old World sense of caregiving among American men and women, I'm equally nostalgic for the thoughts and language of those Sixties feminists who argued for finding "new forms," because change can come only from fresh ways of thinking about this complicated dilemma.

Janet Giele's thoughtful analysis of temperance women and suffragettes presents an interesting analogy for today's political and cultural divide. A broadly based feminist coalition can be built if it first and foremost includes women's interests as wives and mothers and makes national health insurance and paid parental leave two of its key issues. Old and new feminist leaders must be sympathetic to how cultural values help define women's choices. By better reconciling the interconnection and inherent tensions between ethnicity and feminism, between cultural systems that value familial dependence and the American search for personal autonomy, we can begin to understand ourselves more fully as daughters, wives, and mothers.

By economically valuing dependency work, we will increase respect for this difficult job that has traditionally been unpaid or poorly paid. A social revolution must be broad enough to include the women whom we hire to care for our children. Caregivers need to receive a fair wage, benefits, and Social Security, and work within a defined job description. If they are hired to cuddle, feed, bathe, and play with the child while the parent is absent, they shouldn't be ordered, as some employers feel is within their right, to scrub the kitchen floor.

I have listened to dozens of nannies who have a diary full of troubling stories, but the words of one woman hired to care for a young girl stayed with me: "Every day there would be a new note. Clean the refrigerator. Clean the bathroom. Do the laundry. Take the shoes to the shoemaker. Take the wine-glasses out of the cabinets and clean them. Do the grocery shopping. I didn't have time to sit for a minute. I saved every one of those notes. I saved them for my daughter. I want her to know the importance of going to school and getting an education. I want something better for her life."

Yesterday's reformers who sought a higher social morality can serve as a guide for a new generation of women leaders. Let's not, of course, imitate their moral superiority; zealotry doomed the temperance movement and led the unenlightened rest to want to drown their inferior selves with a stiff bootlegged drink. But the early reform movements applied the universal feeling of a mother toward her child to public policy: My child, and therefore all children, must be treated fairly; and freedom of opportunity should not be earned by the exploitation of someone else.

* * *

Home is where one starts from. As we grow older
The world becomes stranger, the pattern more complicated
Of dead and living. Not the intense moment
Isolated, with no before and after.
But a lifetime burning in every moment. . .

—T. S. ELIOT, *FOUR QUARTETS*

As the years went by, I yearned for the slow drawl of boredom, hugged it like a favorite old friend. For boredom brought me closer, I imagined, to living in time, my eye on the interminable minute hand instead of recognizing the moment well after it passed, that painful longing of fingering old photographs. If I could accept boredom—that incongruity between my interests and another's desires—then I could savor the moment until it slipped away like any other.

Early one Saturday morning, Michael set up a scene of his favorite Playmobil characters, little plastic figures that commandeer ambulances, garbage and fire trucks, cranes, planes, and automobiles. On this morning, he huddled together two police figures for a meeting. A robber stole a dollar from a bank and didn't give it back. The police considered whether to put him in jail or give him two tickets. The characters decided, my son told me, to give him two tickets that cost three dollars. Justice delivered, and I sit back pondering, à la the child psychology of Robert Coles, the inherent morality of four-year-olds.

For years we played with these plastic figures almost every day. My son's stuffed animals also became characters in the scene, waiting to be rescued if their house was on fire or they were in need of an ambulance. The animals were called "the friends," and it was my job to hold these furry creatures while my son directed the action. This play, which could last for hours, was both interminably boring and sublimely wonderful. Between the action of colliding vehicles and valiant rescues, we discussed his friends, good and bad dreams, preschool and kindergarten; piece by piece, bits of his day emerged, and his moral and social dilemmas unfolded.

For better or for worse, I have fixed my steady maternal gaze upon this child, my only child, in a life certainly different from the Italian mothers of my past who were busily cooking, sewing, or cleaning while their children played with siblings and cousins. Ironically, perhaps my approach is nearer to the sentiments of many women in Italy today who are thoroughly indulgent of their one child (at least as my Italian friends describe and director Nanni Moretti humorously depicted in his autobiographical film *Caro Diario*). Holding my son's animal friends, watching the action, I understood that this moment would pass to the next as quickly as I had folded away shirts too small, pants too tight.

If I knew how quickly the years flew by, would I have savored standing by his crib, swinging the mobile to those chubby arms and legs, instead of imagining anyplace but here? Or maybe it is impossible for someone like me—who believed that adulthood meant autonomy and independence, and lives in a city where social activities, even gathering with friends, requires rigorous planning—to enjoy spending hours alone entertaining someone who hasn't learned to speak. Perhaps I am able to appreciate this time only through the filtered glow of nostalgia.

We seek autonomy, but we long for lasting relationships; we search for clear-cut answers when certainty can't exist. How could the gleefully self-assertive college graduate who demands life without limitations comprehend the complicated patterns of middle age? Will we ever detect, in large ways or small, the effects of each decision we make on one another, or how our collective choices impact the lives of others? How in the shadow of forty years of female opportunity do women like Nidia live, when memories of their sons' and daughters' childhood are blurred images of a time that passed them by.

When Mary Met Livia

HOW TO STIR A LITTLE DEPENDENCY INTO THE SAUCE

Mary loves travel. Livia says there's no place like home.
Change excites Mary. Livia fears it.
Mary embraces her independence. Livia insists upon familial dependence.
Mary is childless. Livia is an Italian mother.

O**KAY, LADIES**, it's time for a meet and greet. Inner Mary Tyler Moore, say hello to inner Livia Soprano, that archetypical Italian mother. Shake hands, and please try not to hurt each other. Because I know you're both there, parts of me, my daughter/mother, Old World/New World selves. One side has been practiced, studied, and earned through hard work, my American cultural diploma. The other side has been handed down through child rearing and genetics, the DNA evidence I've stashed in the closet. My cultural diploma has taken me around the world, placed me in thrilling and threatening situations; my DNA evidence, on the other hand, surfaces as I age, and it can cause a panic attack in a situation as mundane as getting off at the wrong subway station.

Once I became a mother, Livia swooped down and took her seat at the kitchen table, offering advice over coffee and *tatalles*, even when I didn't ask. Travel, change, independence each represented risk, she warned, and I needed safety.

So when my son was a toddler, I turned down opportunities to travel to other cities. I said that the costs of child care would consume much of what I would earn on those trips. But that was merely an excuse—I couldn't abide the thought of getting on a plane and leaving my family. Venturing out alone in the world frightened me in a way it never did before; I could enjoy these trips only with my husband and son, sharing adventures, protecting my child in order to protect myself. Providing care created a space for me into which fear temporarily dissipated; the large hand that wraps the smaller one gains the strength to push away the dangers of the unknown.

As my son grows older, Mary is slowly reappearing after her years-long hiatus. She wasn't around much when diapers needed changing and spit happened (as those cute little bibs used to say), and she avoided playgrounds at all costs with their tedious, high-pitched negotiations over who claimed the sand shovel. But seeing more of her lately has certainly been good for my own sense of self and my ability to take on new challenges. Mary is much more presentable in public than poor Livia in her shapeless old housedress, so the social pressure to bring Mary back weighs heavily in her favor.

But I can't entirely abandon Livia and the steadfastness she offered in those early years. Despite her all-too-familiar messages of guilt and self-pity, of fear and fatalism, she was one powerful matriarch. And the Italian mothers whom I have loved, those wonderfully impossible matriarchs, have also been—and this is where they permanently part company from Livia—ethical women who, if they didn't exactly enjoy la dolce vita, lived in sync with the rhythms and rituals of the seasons, and spent most of the hours of the day in close proximity to their children.

Throughout the years, they have never wanted to disappoint, with their strong and sometimes strange determination. My eighty-five-year-old mother, temporary blinded in one eye when a bottle of Clorox toppled off the washing machine and splashed her face, returned home at one in the morning after a Saturday evening spent in the emergency room and proceeded to clean the turkey she promised to cook her family for Sunday dinner. My aunt, despite breaking her hip right before the holiday season, insisted upon preparing the traditional Christmas Eve fish dinner. Leaning on her walker, her kitchen utensils tied to each side, she simmered the eel and sautéed the squid. These women, loyal soldiers on the domestic battlefront, have written their own rule book of duty and dedication.

By leaving the Old World, my ancestors allowed me to embrace the New World's most precious gifts: individual freedoms, universal education, and an order in the world that places women alongside men. I welcomed—indeed, felt saved by—the New World's freer hand that offered the means and opportunities to experience life outside the confines of custom. As a midwestern newspaper noted in the 1920s, "in the minds of many there is quite a difference between the man of spaghetti and the Puritan and Cavalier."

But if my Old and New World sides could at least hear each other out, understand from whence they came, maybe they could negotiate a sustainable mix of self and selflessness. For I call upon these Italian mammas when the frantic charge of modern life makes me yearn for what I find missing in contemporary American culture: a deep-rooted ethic of care, a belief in human beings as something other than human capital, and a view of life that isn't first and foremost shaped by economic transactions.

I cringed, for example, reading Linda R. Hirshman's published response to the decision made by more and more highly educated women to stay home and raise their children (the magazine article, in the liberal *American Prospect*, was later turned into a book-length feminist manifesto called *Get To Work*). "The family," Hirshman wrote, "with its repetitious, socially invisible, physical tasks—is a necessary part of life, but it allows fewer opportunities for full human flourishing than public spheres like the market or the government."

Hirshman offered a rational marketplace solution to solving the delicate problems of growing up, raising children, and finding satisfying and flexible work. Faulting the decision of many women to major in the liberal arts ("the purpose of a liberal education is not, with the exception of a minuscule number of academic positions, job preparation"), she argued that soon after college women must focus on finding the money. "Money is the marker of success in a market economy," Hirshman explained, "it usually accompanies power, and it enables the bearer to wield power, including within the family."

To Hirshman, the family—"repetitious, socially invisible," with (God help us) "physical tasks"—provides neither emotional nor spiritual satisfaction; it's merely necessary. Welcome to the twenty-first century, in which Americans have learned to commodify every aspect of our lives, including how we care for our children and aging parents.

Whenever I travel to western Europe, I encounter in basic and simple ways an alternative rhythm, one not exclusively defined by the goal of continual economic profit. I wonder whether this different sense of one's day-to-day self is the real appeal of all those escape fantasies about spending a year in Tuscany or Provence. Many Europeans, appropriately skeptical of the idea that happiness is best found in the marketplace, seem to embody the truism that one should work to live rather than live to work.

Walking into a small chocolate store in Spain, I inquire about several types of bars, and a worker opens all of them for me to taste. Three wrapped bars of chocolate! He just lost a few euros' worth of business in an act that could get him fired in America. And how can I forget the Venetian glassmaker who left me alone with his expensive hand-blown jewelry in order to deliver an espresso to his mamma?

The ethic of care is deeply ingrained in Italian life, personally and publicly. Nurturing (or what Americans might call coddling) is a strong part of the elementary school ethos. Children have the same teacher for the first five years who assumes the role of mother-educator, holding little hands and intuitively understanding her students' forming character while teaching the fundamentals. The children address the teacher by his or her first name and everyone speaks in the informal "*tu.*" An Italian woman I met was surprised to discover that American public schools change teachers every year.

"I asked my brother why this is the case," she told me, "and he said that Americans must teach their children not to have a deep sense of ties. They need to be able to pull away and take a job, if they like, at the other end of your country."

Italian parents are expected to care for their children until they are economically self-sufficient, no matter how old their children may be. This cultural norm was challenged a few years ago when a divorced father from Florence went to court seeking to end support for a son in his thirties and a younger daughter. The court agreed about the son but said that the father had to continue to pay two hundred euros a month to the daughter, twenty-eight at the time and still in college.

The papa protested, and the mamma took the daughter's side. After a series of appeals, Italy's highest court finally ruled in the father's favor in 2006 (the daughter was unemployed, depressed after concluding her university studies). Gianna Schelotto, a well-known psychologist, commented on the importance of the court's ruling, saying that decisions by past judges to support children until forty were excessive. By thirty, the psychologist said, children needed to rely less upon their parents and value their own strength: "When you're thirty, it's better to get going."

Compared to this *abbondanza* of Italian family support, the United States is at the other end of the spectrum, believing that dependence is always a pejorative word. Even when my son was in kindergarten, other mothers would tell me about the importance of giving our boys a sense of independence. "But he's only five," I would secretly moan.

Yet as we take pride in our independence, and that of our

children, snickering at the idea of being ordered by an Italian court to hand over two hundred euros a month to a "child" in her late twenties, it's worth remembering that the college education for this man's children was, except for a nominal fee, paid for (along with their health care) entirely by the government. American parents, or their children, are saddled with tens of thousands of dollars in school loans and debt, and parents often carry for years the high costs of health care extension plans. "It's really quite suffocating," commented an Italian friend who teaches at a New Jersey college. "Graduating college and burdened with debt, these children are unprepared to take care of themselves."

After our centuries-long fascination, and fixation, with achieving independence—"that freedom that starts so early in the States," as Wilde-Menozzi writes, "where a mother and father want you to become . . . to go"—psychologists are now entertaining the possibility of a healthy side to dependency. "Only in recent years," an article in the science section of the *New York Times* reported, "have researchers begun to realize that while in some guises dependence can undermine mental health, in others it can provide valuable social support."

According to one study, for example, college students who scored higher in measures of dependency had significantly better grade point averages than their more independent peers. The study's authors theorized that the dependent students excelled because they were much more likely to seek out a professor's help. Used to a strong familial support structure, the students were comfortable reaching out for assistance when on their own. Despite this fresh revelation about dependency, the verdict was still out as to whether these traits nourished or smothered relationships in the long run.

Researchers, seeking to determine whether people have "dependency traits," rated respondents by how strongly they agreed with a long list of statements, which began with the following assertions:

"I constantly try, **and very often go out of my way**, to please or help people I am close to."

"**Being isolated** from others is bound to lead to unhappiness."

"It is important to be **liked and approved of** by others."

If strong agreement with these three statements is a clue to my psyche, then I must raise my hand and admit "I am a dependent person." But after my initial inclination to sneak off and enter a twelve-step dependency rehab program, I began to wonder, who doesn't go out of their way to please or help the people they love? Who wants to live an isolated life? These traits—wanting to please loved ones, needing to maintain strong social relationships and support—strike me as deeply Italian, but also simply human. And most people would find them positive, unless we wish to become the next Donald Trump, embodying George Orwell's description of capitalist success: "a free-for-all in which the worst man wins."

Still, women will feel ambivalent, or at times deeply angry, when we give of ourselves to care for others but don't believe that others reciprocate with a similar selflessness. Given my family history, I feel particularly vulnerable to the notion of maternal sacrifice, and I wondered whether other ethnic women struggle with similar issues. Curious about the ways in which culture reveals itself in nurturing, I asked Italian-American and Italian women about how their ethnicity was manifested in their day-to-day mothering. And from these discussions, two distinct themes emerged: food and fear.

Women spoke about how much they wanted to cook for their children, teach them about food, and share it communally, relishing the idea of celebrating rituals and holidays with friends or family, and making sure that tables were abundantly filled with traditional dishes. Some talked about how fears about their children's safety clouded their maternal happiness, and how they worried that expressing joy would only lead to losing it, the nagging ache of when "the other shoe will drop."

Listening to their stories, I couldn't help but think about how food and fear are dual symbols of a culture whose members are likely to score extremely high in "dependency traits." Because dependent people are afraid of losing relationships, researchers tell us, they tend to be more compliant and loving. Italian-American women go out of their way to please with aromatic sauces simmering in pots and platters of ravioli, creamy cheeses, and slices of salty prosciutto; like other "traditional" peoples we resist isolation, finding extraordinary comfort in social relationships and extended family. And we are deeply skeptical that the outside world is safe.

Even those who might suffer the most, or be considered outcast, from traditional family values seek ways to stay attached. Serafina, a teacher and single mother of seven-year-old Nicolas, or Nico, describes the struggles she has faced trying to maintain family ties and traditions despite the fact that her lifestyle was initially condemned by her parents. Serafina is the daughter of immigrants who left their hometown of Mola di Bari in 1954 to settle in Brooklyn. When she was forty-three, unmarried and pregnant, Serafina dreaded calling her father to break the news that she was going to have the baby and the child's father had no intention of marrying her. Her papa didn't disappoint; his burst of rage confirmed her worst expectations.

Serafina worked hard to heal wounds—and decided to begin by gathering and feeding her entire family. When Nico was eight months old, she hosted a baptism party in a banquet hall, inviting her Italian relatives as well as Nico's Puerto Rican father and his family. Wine flowed, prosciutto and melon commenced a multi-course feast, and a disc jockey played dance songs throughout the night. The sight of the mother and child dressed in white, along with the grandeur of the event, moved even the sternest heart. "So beautiful, Serafina," one relative commented. "It was an Immaculate Conception."

And Serafina too was content. Although she recognized the fissured life she leads—a modern woman who must nod and smile at a relative's passing remark about an Immaculate Conception—still the baptism gave her the religious ceremony that she desired and the presence of her large extended family. She has since repaired her relationship with her father, who is now her chief supporter and protector. He made the down payment on a condo she recently purchased, and her parents watch Nico on the many days that Serafina needs help. "My son needs to know the importance of family and love," she told me. "He needs to know who he is and where he came from. Even if it's dysfunctional, it's okay."

. . .

ITALIAN WOMEN can be masters of giving, which helps them win the continual love of children, relatives, and neighbors. In Italy, my cousin Maria tells me how her women friends get up at the crack of dawn to prepare the *ragù* and boil the spaghetti for their teenage sons' school lunch before going off to work, and how another friend makes cakes and sweets not only for her beloved sons but the whole class and basketball team, thereby spreading her "motherly love."

I laugh at her Italian mamma stories until I stop to remind myself that every weekday morning for the past six years I have been spreading ricotta cheese on crackers, carefully topping them with fresh shavings of parmigiano or percorino romano, so my son can enjoy his favorite snack along with the sandwich I prepare for his lunch box. This morning preparation is certainly not as extensive as making *pasta con pomodoro*, but it stems from the same impulse.

When Michael was in preschool and kindergarten, I occasionally brought trays of these cheese crackers to school to share with his classmates while I read them Tomie de Paola's *Watch Out for the Chicken Feet in Your Soup*. One of my favorite children's books, it tells the story of a boy embarrassed about visiting his Italian-American grandmother with his blond American friend because she threw their coats atop bowls of bread dough to quicken the leavening process, and served them the weird dish of soup with chicken feet in it.

"My mother used to slap two slices of bologna on bread," my husband reminds me, amused and mystified that anyone would take out a grater and make cheese curls before breakfast. He also can't understand why I sometimes prepare two meals for dinner—one for us and another for our son—because Tony grew up with the motto "If you don't like it, don't eat it." Tony thinks I'm being selfless, but I think there's a selfish gene at work here too. I'm trying to pass along, and preserve, a piece of my Mediterranean culture, seeking intimate communication with my son through food.

"Food was everything," Ann tells me, who is the same age as I am and also a third-generation Italian-American. "It was love. It was comfort. My father considered it part of my education." When Ann told her parents she was marrying a Jewish man who was a restaurateur, her father couldn't have been more pleased, believing that her future husband's career one-upped the choice of her previous boyfriend, a medical student.

"This is better than a doctor!" he proclaimed. "I'm going to have a son-in-law who feeds me well."

Ann was beside herself when her first child, who is now twenty, refused to eat anything she made. Part of his rigidity toward food, she discovered years later, was related to his Asperger's syndrome, but at the time she was saddened and bewildered. "How could I not serve him pastina when he was sick? I had to come up with a Plan B."

How else could she pass on her distinct cultural inheritance? She turned to laundry. "I cared so much about laundry. It was because of the way my grandmother took care of us. She starched our shirts, made them perfect. Even the way I make a bed is how my grandmother taught me." Like her seamstress grandmother, Ann loves to caress fabric, meticulously brushing away wrinkles and folding corners, making small presents out of tumble-dried cloth. Today with her son in college and daughter in high school, Ann gives them lessons on folding laundry, hoping to pass along her grandmother's handiwork. "To me, laundry is about nurturing. It means that somebody loves you, somebody did that for you—someone who wants your pants creased nicely."

My cousin Michelle tells me that she's "over the moon" when her two-year-old son Robert eats and enjoys something she's cooked, and she's "personally hurt when he doesn't. He's in the kitchen with me all the time. He has a step stool for reaching the counters, his own apron, and set of utensils, and he knows how to add a pinch of salt and roll dough. He helps me make dinner or dessert almost every day. He won't need his own play kitchen because he already knows how to use our 'real' one."

Michelle, who has a Ph.D. in anthropology but chose not to work full-time while raising her toddler son and infant daughter, remarked how her half-French husband and fellow anthropologist passes along his cultural interest in growing and preparing food. Having spent his boyhood summers with his family in France, and seeing how most of the food on the family table was either harvested or hunted, he's already teaching his toddler how to garden.

"I knew from the start that food would be my thing with my kids," said Michelle.

A friend who is a book editor recalled teaching her three-year-old son how to make his first smoothie: "'You know why it's good?' I asked him. 'It has yogurt and milk and banana and jam in it. But most important, it's good because you made it yourself.' And I sounded just like those relatives in Naples for whom homemade is always best."

My friend Edi and I commiserate about the deep sense of failure we feel when our sons won't eat vegetables. We can get our boys to eat carrots only by cooking them in chicken stock; therefore, a pot of soup seems to perpetually simmer on our stoves. I make the same soup that my mother first prepared each time her grandson came to visit, a dish Michael loved so much that for years she was known only as Grandma Soup. ("And how's Grandma Sue?" Michael's preschool teacher would ask me. I was left momentarily befuddled as to who this American-sounding, quilt-making grandmother could be.)

Edi's husband, who doesn't share her food obsession, teases her that when he comes home from work she tells him everything their son Matteo ate that day. "I have a full-time job," Edi, a college professor, explained. "I'm working on three books, but my greatest accomplishment is that Matteo ate three peas."

"It's very Catholic," she added, "the idea of putting a piece of food in someone else's mouth."

Every summer Edi travels to Sicily, where she was born, with her American husband and two children because it's important for her to make Italy, as she puts it, their second skin: "My daughter thought that lemons grow in the dirt. There was something very violent about that for me—that you don't know where things grow. . . . When you are disconnected from how things grow, you are disconnected from how people grow."

Reflecting upon the differences between raising her daughter Emily, now eighteen, and eight-year-old Matteo, Edi recalled an Italian incantation between mother and child that contains an essential question of the self. *Di chi sei? Di chi sei?* (Who do you belong to?), the mother repeats. When her daughter was young, Edi, fearful of passing along her heritage of female self-lessness, taught Emily to answer, "I belong to myself."

Years later, Matteo learned a different response. "I belong della mamma, della dada, della sister," he would say in his mixture of English and Italian. The daughter is taught to be self-sufficient, while the son is doted upon and cherished by the family. Yet self-sufficiency can also be preparation for serving others. By age five, Emily could dress and feed herself while Matteo still is "the little prince of the house." And today, Emily loves to cook dinner for friends and brings trays of cookies to her high school.

Whenever I talk with Italian-American women about the ways in which we balance our Old and New World selves, I am struck by our shared sensibilities—how the decades or century since our families settled here have left their traces in the air we breathe. We value the Italian ethic of care but fear of giving of ourselves until nothing is left; we discuss dysfunctional pasts yet acknowledge the sacred and ethical pieces that coexisted with the craziness. I seek out these women because our common traits and quirks affirm my sense of identity, making me feel less isolated and alone. And maybe even a little calmer when that dark marker of Italian-American culture inevitably appears—the terror of how quickly and irrevocably life can take the wrong turn. One of my cousins spoke about how a pervasive fear can undermine her joys daily, and surface even in benign banter.

"There was a girl who worked with me and if you asked how she or her children were, she'd always respond, 'Everything is just wonderful, my children are beautiful and healthy.' I found myself making the sign of the cross to protect her children since she hadn't the sense to do so herself! I've never allowed myself to rave about what my child is doing—in fact, I'm always adding a disclaimer. I always feel as if something unpleasant will follow if you allow those spirits to know how happy you feel. I wonder if Italians originated the practice of knocking on wood."

"Not a day goes by without my seeing my grandmother in my mothering," Ann tells me. She feels she's inherited, along with her grandmother's love of folding laundry, her anxieties. "I am afraid of change. I'm afraid of adventure. When my kids embark on something new, it's really hard for me." Although she continually checks herself, trying not to pass along her fears to her children, Ann still can't overcome her white-knuckled ritual on an airplane: "When the wheels first take off from the ground, I have to make the sign of the cross."

Serafina admits that her mother would be happiest if her daughter never left the house, a sentiment I well understand because my mom's motto could be American Express's "Don't Leave Home Without It" minus the "Without It."

"You know how I hate New York" is my mother's stock description of the city in which I've lived for the past three decades. Once, checking in with my mom while I was on vacation, she spent the entire conversation repeating the details of a true life crime show she had just seen about a child abduction. After retelling the story, she cheerfully concluded, "Have a great vacation!" and hung up the phone.

Serafina and her mother argue about adverse weather conditions: "It's snowing. I hope you're not going out with Nico."

"Mom, I'm going out with Nico *because* it's snowing."

"Such a strong wind," she declares a few weeks later. "You're not taking Nico out in this wind, are you?"

"Mom, what do you think?"

"Ah, *camenamond*," Serafina's mother utters resignedly in her Molese dialect.

Cammina il mondo. You are a walker of the world.

For those daughters, granddaughters, and great-grand-daughters of immigrants who have desired to become walkers of the world against the wishes of our parents, we pay a large emotional price. I asked Rose Fichera McAloon, a Sicilian-born psychologist and founder of the Italian-American

Psychotherapy Center, which runs workshops on anxiety, separation, and fear—the antipasti to many Sunday family meals—why Italian-Americans seemed more fearful to me than other assimilated Americans. McAloon, who also holds a doctorate in Italian literature from Columbia, believes that every individual has his or her own psychological struggle, but she distinguishes between this personal anguish and a broader choice to view the world as either benign or dangerous.

The challenge for many Italian-Americans, as McAloon sees it, is to live beyond the metal wires of a self-imprisoning fence, to unlearn the message spoon-fed since childhood—that danger lurks around every corner. "I'd like to talk about the Italian-American psyche as if it's unique. It's not," she told me, speculating on the origins of this fear. "It's a lower- and working-class outlook that comes out of poverty."

McAloon certainly is right in suggesting that more prosperous societies can help people experience greater pleasure and suffer fewer fears by offering economic opportunities and combating illness and diseases. But could this timidity stem only from the pernicious effects of southern Italian poverty passed along to the generations that settled here? Why have many northern Italians I've met possessed a similar cautiousness? And the descendants of northern European coal miners and peasant farmers don't seem to be leaping from table to table to find enough wood upon which to knock. The Protestant ethic finds weakness in fear, demands denial of fear. It's an ethic that, as a Protestant friend commented to me, can leave one with a feeling of false safety—an equally distorted sense.

There seems something particularly powerful about Mediterranean fatalism—originating in the classical belief that everything in life is dictated by orders directly from above—and its accompanying desire to keep the surrounding chaos and evil at bay. While the rational mind coolly calculates the odds in its favor, the fatalistic one stays fearfully on guard, looking to the heavens for signals. (Consider the difference between passengers on a British Air jet and those on Alitalia. One plane reaches the runway in London and everyone quietly disembarks; the other lands in Rome to a burst of applause, praising the miracle of wheels touching the ground.)

"My mother's favorite phrase was '*Sta attenta*,' be careful," Rose McAloon tells me. "I had to make a conscious decision. Instead of saying 'Be careful' to my sons, I'd say, 'Have fun.' "

I, too, try to substitute a nonchalant "Have fun" when my heart pounds "Be careful," knowing how easily fear passes through the generations, and how a mother's fear can become an overpowering force in her child's life, not to mention her own. When fear controls, every decision becomes a potential mistake; the channel for joy is choked, opened only through the sigh of a regret avoided.

Or as my friend Edi put it, "Fear is a kind of food. It goes inside you, as food does."

And perhaps it derives from the same source: food and fear as by-products of dependency, from a culture known for its cuisine and one that believes that not until thirty is it time "to get going," from a people who go out of their way to please and rely strongly on one another for social, psychological, and economic support. Or, more generously speaking, a country that values *interdependence*, as an Italian journalist once corrected me, raising a dark brow appalled and astonished that I would characterize his country as steeped in dependency traits. Yet scoring high in measures of dependency probably means figuring out sooner than more independent types—like the British and their American sisters—that a good meal is necessary for communal pleasure, and maybe even keeping someone home a little bit longer.

In the United States, on the other hand, newspapers run an item each fall about "national family dinner night," a specially earmarked evening to share a meal together. (Will a Hallmark card follow?) A television commercial features a son calling his mother to ask whether he can stay over at a friend's house for dinner. The woman, dumbfounded that any family could eat together on a weeknight, insists upon speaking to the friend's mother to make sure her son is telling the truth. And, yes, a real mother takes the phone and declares that she has a delicious, nutritious dinner awaiting—a big bucket of Kentucky Fried Chicken. Who has time for the slow preparation of food? Parents working long hours can't also be expected to shop for, and put together, a balanced home-cooked meal every night.

Besides, those large, greasy buckets of fried chicken are an essential component of the government's metrics to determine American economic strength—the drumstick and thigh expenditures that compose our Gross Domestic Product. As journalist Jonathan Rowe points out, when we talk about the economy growing, what we mean is that we have increased the overall amount of what we produce. But the goods that the government calculates are only those that can be measured in dollars (the "good" of a parent caring for a child doesn't get counted). Since the 1940s, the American government has been obsessed with increasing the size of our Gross Domestic Product—and similarly, we ridicule European countries for their inability to grow their economy as large as ours. Yet our government has consistently failed to consider the overall effects of the expenditures we make, or how those expenditures might supplant more desirable aims.

Many things that make up family life don't get counted in the Gross Domestic Product, but expenditures that can damage the fabric of a family do. Parents who cook, spend time talking with their children, and take a leisurely after-dinner walk contribute less to our GDP than those who drive SUVs to fast-food restaurants and drop their kids off at a video arcade. The parents who spend less money than their more commercial counterparts, argues Rowe, "are threats to the economy as portrayed by the GDP. By that standard, the best kids are the ones who eat the most junk food and exercise the least, because they will run up the biggest medical bills for obesity and diabetes. This assumption has been guiding our economic policies for the past sixty years at least. Is it surprising that the family structure is shaky, real community is in decline, and children have become petri dishes of market-related dysfunction and disease?"

So it's KFC, Mickey D's, and Burger King—the international signature of our fast-moving, profit-making, independent life.

• • •

ARE THERE lessons to be garnered from "the men of spaghetti," from cultures that encourage dependency traits, other than how to enjoy the great indoors and prepare a tasty *ragù*? Dependent cultures may also help guide us in redirecting values tilted heavily to the dictates of the marketplace.

A dancer friend described how she was invited some years back to talk to a group of women at Barnard, her alma mater, about starting a career and creating her own small dance company. After discussing her work, she said as an aside, "Oh yeah—it also helps if you fall in love and marry a guy who has a steady job so he can provide the health insurance."

Silence.

"It was the elephant in the room," she told me. "Everyone glared at me. I couldn't believe how angry they were."

Her terrible faux pas was to admit that she was dependent on a man she loved to provide her with health insurance, which had been too costly to acquire on her own. The Barnard women, on the other hand, were furious that she had placed herself in this traditional female role, admitting financial support from marriage, rather than sharing exhilarating tales of economic independence. But if the government doesn't offer health insurance, and the many jobs my friend held to support herself as a dancer—personal trainer, extra on a soap opera, dance troupe performer for bar mitzvahs and weddings—didn't either, then should she have abandoned her desires and taken a nine-to-five job on feminist principle? That might solve the dependency-on-husband issue, but it could also mean fewer dancers, poets, and painters, not to mention having to endure duller bar mitzvahs.

Our collective societal wish for independence, that longing to get government off our backs, has helped put us in this position, yet women get blamed for the inherent lack of options, glared at for relying upon a man. By feeding this myth of independence, shuddering at the notion of the "welfare state," we continue to strip government of its essential role—to serve and protect without the distorting motive of profit. Insisting upon tax cuts guarantees that government can never provide health insurance, or a college education, or paid-leave time—all benefits offered by most western European governments.

A similar reasoning problem exists when discussing the options for working and stay-at-home mothers. The decisions that women make, as Joan Williams remarked, are usually based upon "the choices they have, not what they should have." Choices, that is, derived from market concerns, not about the well-being of women and their families.

"[Mothers] can be away from home and see their children before they fall asleep," said Williams. "Or they can work part-time or reduced hours in a very punitive atmosphere or they can drop out of the workforce. The choices that mothers make with these three options might be different if they had a real choice, not a false choice. If they had a choice to cut back their hours or reduce them without marginalization, they might. Many women who are at home might add paid work to their lives, if they had a real choice." A recent Pew Research Center survey seems to confirm Williams's hunch: The majority of working and stay-at-home mothers say they would prefer to work part-time.

Just as psychologists are exploring the healthy sides of dependency in personal relationships, a similar perspective needs to be extended to civic life. By taking a lesson from Old World cultures, accepting that personal and professional choices can lead to periods of dependency, and that at times we all need assistance (Leave behind those dependency management programs! Celebrate Dependence Day!), we can search for that inner mamma and tap her indomitable will.

Reason of Age

How surprising news is learned about the Venetian glassmaker

Often I'd think about my glassmaker acquaintance and his delivering a cup of espresso to his mother, a gesture that during an American workday would only raise an eyebrow and evoke a patronizing smile. I also missed seeing his elegant artistry, so one day I decided to look for his work in New York. Roaming through a museum store that the glassmaker told me carried his jewelry, I found a familiar-looking pendant on display and asked an employee about it.

"Do you know the artist?" he inquired.

"Not really," I replied. "I met him when I was in Italy last summer and admired his work. Why do you ask?"

"Well, we lost him for a while. He was traveling in India during the tsunami."

"Oh my God—is he okay?"

"Yes, we think so. He was found in a local hospital."

It was difficult for me to fathom that this man, whom I had randomly met in Italy, was swept up in a colossal human tragedy of our age, the tsunami in Southeast Asia. I hoped that his life was saved. I had felt a cultural connection and affection toward him that made the story harder to bear as this strange turn of events pulsed through my head. Once again I was forced to recognize how this life of ours passively, violently curls, bearing us up with it and throwing us down with it along the way.

Surely not all is for the best in the best of all possible worlds, as Voltaire, the patron saint of the Enlightenment, contended in his satire *Candide*. Voltaire was mocking the optimistic philosophers of his age, and their belief in a God with a divine hand in all human affairs, as he sought to tease meaning from the random cruelty of the 1755 Lisbon earthquake, which destroyed three-quarters of the city and set off a tsunami. Indeed, if any event broke the yoke of the Old World, raising profound questions about the ancient codes to which Europeans had been bound and opening people's minds to Enlightenment thinking, it was the Lisbon tsunami.

But Voltaire's insistence that the ultimate ends of men were at all times the same, and that reason alone would offer the means to a better life, providing the tools to unearth what human beings truly wanted, found its limitations several centuries after it was adopted as the defining philosophy of our age. Despite all the advances of science, the twenty-first-century tsunami destroyed with the same force and impunity as the Lisbon disaster. The waves wiped away the belief that a rational world could outsmart nature, that the luxury resorts of Phuket would be better protected than fishing villages in India.

We're still left with the same meaning-of-life questions that plagued Voltaire and the *philosophes*. And today when Western philosophers—rather than scientists or Monty Python—tackle that question of questions, their response reflects the spirit of the Enlightenment and its individualist bias. A meaningful life, said English philosopher John Cottingham, is "one in which the individual is engaged . . . in genuinely worthwhile activities that reflect his or her rational choice as an autonomous agent."

Reflecting on Cottingham's definition, Terry Eagleton observes, "None of this is false . . . [but] it does not see the meaning of life as a common or reciprocal project. It fails to register that there can be by definition no meaning, whether of life or anything else, which is unique to myself alone. If we emerge into being in and through one another, then this must have strong implications for the meaning-of-life question."

Shall we begin with a cup of espresso?

．　．　．

I HAVE NEVER been tempted, despite my long devotion to individual liberty, to march with those who, in its name, reject adherence to a particular nation, community, culture, tradition, language—the myriad unanalysable strands that bind men into identifiable groups," wrote Isaiah Berlin, whose philosophy has guided me through this book. "This seems to me noble but misguided. When men complain of loneliness, what they mean is that nobody understands what they are saying. To be understood is to share a common past, common feelings and language, common assumptions, the possibility of intimate communication—in short, to share common forms of life. This is an essential human need: to deny this is a dangerous fallacy. . . . Such criticisms as I have made of the doctrines of the Enlightenment and of its lack of sympathy for emotional bonds between members of races and cultures, and its idealistic but hollow doctrinaire internationalism, spring, in my case, from this almost instinctive sense of one's own roots."

What does it mean to be an in-between person trying to sort out the conflicting messages of heredity and culture? Can one find the appropriate space between a family-centered Old World culture that threatens the loss of self and an individual-oriented New World culture in which we're lost in self? Can I ever free myself from inherited behaviors or personality traits reinforced by this instinctive sense of my own roots?

While some people quietly internalize their feelings about the small rituals that mark any passage of time, I am an emoter. I sobbed at my son's preschool graduation. The other mothers smiled and some chuckled as I tried to suppress the cascade of tears, a response that seemed more appropriate for parents dropping off their child on a college campus than for a juice and cookies gathering of four year olds.

But there I sat ("We have one every year," a teacher told me later. She was trying, I suppose, to make the "one" feel better), watching my little boy with construction paper cat ears attached to his head—his costume for the loose attempt of a play that the class had just performed. The celebration closed with twenty angelic children sitting in a circle singing "Adios Amigos" (until we meet again). When my son looked at me, I smiled widely, but ducking behind my husband and other parents, I wiped my tear-streaked face, knowing that all futures mean accepting an end. I couldn't contain the grief and force of nostalgia, a truth lost on the young, that place and the fabric of our relationships will change or eventually disappear.

"Listening to them singing 'Adios Amigos,'" I recounted to a friend, "I thought, Just go ahead and put the knife through my heart."

"Put the knife through your heart!" He laughed. "You are so Italian."

Two days after preschool graduation (oh, they become postgrads so fast), without considering the effects of this choice, I went to see the director's uncut version of my favorite celluloid bath of nostalgia, *Cinema Paradiso*. The moment the film began, on the first note of Ennio Morricone's mellifluous score, as the camera panned the translucent emerald sea and settled upon a sun-bleached ledge that held a bowl of lemons and a sprig of rosemary, I grabbed for the Kleenex. How quickly I could become the old Sicilian mother in black, waiting to see whether her son, who now lives in Rome and has never returned to the village of his youth, will arrive that day for the funeral of an old friend.

Time is retraced. Now the mother is pretty and slender, holding the hand of her adorable son as they travel through the ancient town's circuitous streets. I am young, old, black or white haired; by morphing time and place, aging decades by the hour, I leave the theater in a puddle, having fully surrendered to the overwhelming power of nostalgia.

And my family isn't even from Sicily.

As a mother, my past longings and constant fears will most likely inform my judgments and decisions. On a scale of maternal overprotectiveness, my needle points to red, the one that says hold on tight. Yet each year also teaches me how to let go a little more and appreciate the beauty that can accompany change. I see how the passage of time shapes my son into the extraordinary person that he continues to become.

Over the years, Michael has heard me tell the preschool graduation story countless times, and he has seen my eyes fill up with joy as well as sadness. At ten, he knows full well the type of mother that I am. When we discuss change and new life stages, Michael teases me about my predisposition to tearfulness.

"Do you think that all I do is cry?" I ask in mock self-defense.

"No," Michael responds, deliberating for a moment. "You cry and then you write about it."

If I have to check myself for traces of the *mamma del sud*, so be it. For I can no longer turn my back on a community and family ethos that requires a measure of sacrifice or simply laugh at the fears of overprotective mammas who know that life is not in our control.

That thorny personal and public dilemma—to reconcile the quest for individual freedom with the need for collective responsibility—will always feel particularly poignant to Old World daughters who become New World mothers. Sipping the earthy wine of my ancestors' southern Italian terrain, imagining my grandfather's hands caressing bunches of grapes as summer turned to fall, I find new meanings in the lessons of my past. Not that leaving the house with wet hair on a chilly day can lead to getting sick (although, to my chagrin, today's research on the common cold concurs with my mother's belief) but that we are deeply connected to one another and need to nurture these ties. Women well understand the power of reason in shaping our lives for the better, but we also need time for the poetry once cultivated in our grandfathers' gardens and space to measure meaning in the singsong of a child.

Acknowledgments

$\mathscr{D}$URING THE YEARS of writing this book, many people have offered an invaluable moral support. I would especially like to thank my mother and my brothers for their love and their devotion. My mother's humor and energy and my brother Henry's enthusiasm continually inspire me. My brother Bob's unflagging encouragement has strengthened me since my childhood, and his gentle spirit brings forth memories of my father. My thanks to my in-laws Sylvia and Earl Shorris, beacons of wisdom and encouragement who always had the right words, even during the toughest times, as well as James Shorris and Cindy Hyatt Shorris. Sylvia, my Mediterranean kindred spirit, particularly understood my preoccupation with the lasting imprints of culture on the self.

I am also extraordinarily grateful to have friends who are

family: Thank you to Jennifer Brown and Vincent Santoro for your love and your laughter; Susan Jacobson and David Moskovitz for your generosity and your insightful stories; Ruth Pastine and Gary Lang for your passion about art and for our many shared days of early child rearing; and LynNell Hancock and Filip Bondy for your wise editorial counsel and frequent sanity checks.

My friends Joanna Clapps Herman, Edvige Giunta, and Wallis Wilde-Menozzi provided invaluable insights into Italian-American and Italian culture (and cooked some delicious meals for me along the way). Stefano Albertini of New York University's Casa Italiana ensured that I didn't get lost in translation.

Thank you, Annette Fuentes, Rob Neuwirth, Dana English, Susan McConnaughy, Jan Carr, and Jill Wright for espresso and sympathy. Jess Taylor read an early version of this manuscript and his insights helped me see the Brazilian forest for the trees; Elisabeth Dyssegaard also offered invaluable editorial ideas. Donna Brodie and the good folks at the Writers Room provided the physical space to work, and my roommates, Jeff Garigliano and Nancy Stout, the psychic space to keep going.

I am so lucky to have Susan Ramer as my agent and my friend. She is my adviser, wise reader, and guardian angel, whose faith in me never wavered.

My editor, Alane Salierno Mason, expanded her family twofold as I wrote this book, yet she still found time to lend her extraordinary editorial gifts and acute understanding of our shared heritage.

My son, Michael, and my husband, Tony, have taught me the infinite dimensions of familial love. When I began thinking about this book, Michael was a preschooler holding my hand, and as I finish writing it, Michael is an amazing child who lends me his hand, offering his formidable computer skills and his copy editor's eye. I know that without the love, encouragement, and hand-holding of my husband, Tony, this book simply would not have been possible. His rational understanding of my irrational spirit helps me balance my Old and New World selves (knock on wood!), and his sensitivity, intelligence, and humor make each day a better one. To both of them—my teachers, my guides—I am forever indebted and grateful; and to them I dedicate this book.